conversations

"We need to remember that across generations that there is as much to learn as there is to teach."

— GLORIA STEINEM

. . .

"If I had one do over I would have to say that I would have worked smarter, not harder. It's a hard question to answer, because I wouldn't have done one particular thing differently, but a mess of little things I would do differently."

— CARLIE

. . .

"... don't be afraid to venture out in the world and make mistakes, that's how you learn and you need to learn from each mistake and move forward."

— ALICE

. . .

"Play is not the opposite of work. It is the attitude with which we enjoy the company of others."

— ROBERTA

. . .

"I would tell a woman my age: be proud, find inspiration in everything you do, give back to those younger than you, and learn from the lessons and mistakes of our elders."

— SUSAN

. . .

"Hope that you have both great joy in your life and great sorrow. Let God lead you through both. With Him your joy will make you beautiful and your sorrow will make you strong."

— LISA

. . .

❖ ❖ ❖

Order this book online at www.trafford.com
or email orders@trafford.com

Most Trafford titles are also available at major online book retailers.

Printed in the United States of America.

ISBN: 978-1-4907-3848-2 (sc)
ISBN: 978-1-4907-3847-5 (e)

Trafford rev. 07/08/2014

 www.trafford.com

North America & international
toll-free: 1 888 232 4444 (USA & Canada)
fax: 812 355 4082

❖ ❖ ❖

conversations
connecting generations of women

Compiled by Karen Gutowsky and Patricia Mesch

❖ ❖ ❖

" It's not what happens to you, but what you do with
what happens to you. It's not what actually happens,
but what you perceive as happening. It's not the
event, but the meaning attached to the event."
–Darcy

preface

The intent of this book is to do two things: to learn from our collective experiences and to encourage using the insights of each other and ourselves in order to move forward in our celebration as women. As we become busier and more fragmented in our society there is a greater need to protect the essence of female companionship across generations. What we have learned from this research is that women's conversations can be nurtured in electronic chat rooms, Bible studies, book groups, kids sporting events, going to lunch, knitting clubs, and neighborhood teas. It is not the physical form or space that is important, rather it is the essence of the conversation. We discovered the unique richness in conversations when generations of women mixed in dialogue.

Conversations with other women results in a lifetime of treasures. We kept each woman's voice intact as each spoke.

" I always love to hear the stories of older women and how they encountered difficulty in their lives and how they overcame that. Hearing advice from seasoned veterans has always been of interest to me."

–Kathryn

If only I had known I would have . . . But would I?

What would you ask an older woman? A 26 year old expectant
Mother responded to our question: "I would not ask for advice,
because who knows if I would listen (I have not in the past).
I would not ask for her opinion, but I would ask her to tell about
her life and I would listen. I would want to hear about her husband,
about her childhood, about her children, about her life adventures,
and I would listen." And a 70 year old woman states that she would
tell a younger woman to "listen to what other women would do
over, listen to what their children say and don't say . . . to try and
understand the mystery of being a woman in America."

There are so many choices for women to make today, yet, are they
any different than what our mothers and grandmothers were
confronted with? Are we supposed to be caretakers or are we
supposed to be an object of desire? Are we supposed to be beautiful,
alluring, intelligent, athletic and professional as well as mothers
and grandmothers who fit a mold? Is the American woman a Daisy
Miller or a Daisy Buchanan or a political icon? Are we supposed to
aspire to being perfect, unattainable as the media often portrays or
are we part of a whole? Is the "whole" family, career, community,
church, country, world? In other words am I really my own self or
am I a part of a whole?

Over and over, in many different ways, women ask these questions,
searching for the answer or wondering if there really is an answer.

In the midst of this we grow up. We go to college, find jobs, some of
us marry, have children and if we don't do all of these we look for
ways to group ourselves in society. In other words we desperately try

to conform yet maintain our identity. Many women struggle and wonder how "she" fits into what the American Woman is supposed to be. In this process many of us become way too dependent, way too independent, way too wild, way too reticent. Many struggle to be known – others to be unknown... but all recognize there IS something to figure out. Religion, Education, Money, Status, Friendships offer respite, but still most of us wonder.

In the course of raising four daughters, studying and teaching I have found my graduate thesis coming back to haunt me. In the act of utterance one comes to meaning... a bit of existential phenomenology... so simple. The more we talk, the more we understand and our lives become easier because understanding occurs... We must talk to each other.

So we did, and here we are with conversations to share with other women. We derived much satisfaction and stimulation from answering the questions we were given. We found it even more stimulating to read other women's perspectives. We discovered that in this global world so many American women are still striving to be whatever it is "we" are supposed to be, and wondering...

Talking with each other makes it so much easier. *We invite you to join the conversation.*

—*Pat's Reflection*

" A very important focus in your life is your
relationships with other people. Nurture them,
believe in them, make time for them, grow with
them."

–Lorraine

" Love yourself, every imperfect part of you,
see life as a journey – not a goal line and
listen/see/feel the beauty and miracles that
surround you to keep you going when times
get tough as well as during those celebratory
moments."

–Susan

part one | stories about: self

what I did right

what I would do over

questions I would ask another woman

what I would tell another woman

and for some – ten years later

in my 20's

" I would tell a younger woman that she can do anything that she wants to, that to really pursue what she wants and to really find something that she enjoys no matter what the challenges are. That intelligence is not everything and appearance is not everything, but love and happiness are everything and that is what she needs to seek, something that she loves and makes her happy!"

–Diana

Carlie

I am 20 years old a senior in college, oldest of two girls, raised by my mother. I am industrious and hard working, majoring in Drama at a Southern University where I received a full scholarship. I have studied in England at a prestigious University. I worked as an intern at a film-writing agency and on the weekends at a high-end retail store. I want to be in movies. I have always wanted this since I was about 3 or 4 years old.

Did "right"— I went to school far away from home. I grew up fast, but fast enough that I know the consequences of my actions. I still act like a child. I still play in the rain, and I still talk on the phone till all odd hours of the night. I live by the motto "make new friends but keep the old" and some people will say that I am overcompensating for something, but I just say that I surround myself with people that hold my past, present, and future. They are good people, and that is why I keep them around. I also give people second, third and fourth chances. Everyone screws up, I know I have, and if I didn't get that second or third chance, who knows where I would be now.

Do "over"— If I had one do over I would have to say that I would have worked smarter, not harder. It's a hard question to answer, because I wouldn't have done one particular thing differently, but a mess of little things I would do differently.

Question asked— What is your best personality trait?

What would you tell— Everyone has good inside. It is your job to look for it, not her job to show it to you. If people constantly went around "Showing" others how good they were, we would be fed up with each other. Get stressed out, it's ok, especially about the little things. Those are the things when you look back, that were big. Learn to love everything. If you think the rain is a horrible inconvenience, go play in it. If you are annoyed sitting in traffic, call someone you haven't talked to in years, just to say hi. Turn your music up really loud, and dance. Be generous with compliments, and stingy with critiques. Critiques may make you feel better immediately, but when no one wants to be around you, you will be asking why, and not a soul will give you an answer for fear of criticism.

—TEN YEARS LATER—

After living on the west coast for 4 years and living in the mid-west for 4 years, I have made really great friends all over the world. I have worked in PR, non profits, and commercial real estate. I have had the BEST bosses, the most wonderful co-workers, and the best roommates. I have made mistakes, learned from them, changed locations, jobs, groups of friends, worked hard, and learned a lot. I live on the east coast and for the first time in a city, I feel at home. I work in fashion and love it. I never thought I would love something as much as I loved acting, but I have learned that being good at something doesn't make it right for you, and as you change, so do your needs from your own day-to-day life. I have friends that are of all different backgrounds, races, genders, and ages. I keep in contact with them, and value them above all else. I talk to family members daily. I try my hardest, and do my best, and try hard not to put too much pressure on myself.

Did "right"— *I tried it all. I still continue to try it all. I am open to failure, because the only failure is, not at least saying you tried. That sounds cheesey, but in all reality, all of my failures have made the things that I value today, hold up against everything else. The ideas of what I expected from myself have melted away, and the new ideas of what I want from my future are dependent on how I feel, not the external items of which I have acquired. I have owned up to my mistakes and tried to make them right. I suit up and show up for the people who need me. I ask for help. I ask for help a lot. I don't worry about my mistakes, but I do worry about repeating them. I learn, and grow, and try to be humble in the best way I know how. I try to make the changes that I have control over, and remember that I am not in* *control of everything. I still live by the motto "make new friends, but keep the old." I stay in touch with people and let everyone know how very much I love them. I don't ask why, but how. The major difference that has become apparent is I have stopped trying so hard to be someone in this world, and I have learned to try to do something in this world every day.*

Do "over"— *If I had one do "over" it would be a general attitude. There is so much expected out of your 20's. I thought my 20's were supposed to be a time where I would find a career that I would be in forever, and grow to a place in it where I would already be respected in my field. I thought I was supposed to find a relationship, get married, and start having kids. I thought I was supposed to be fully financially sound with a plan for retirement, purchasing a house/ condo/apartment. None of those things happened, and that is ok. I would be more open to change. In my 20's I was open to change if it was on my terms, planned by me, and I could control the end result. I have discovered that the best things in life have happened without my knowledge, input, or meddling. I do not regret my choices, but had I been open to the idea of something new, who knows how much the world would have opened up.*

What would you tell— *My best personality trait today is that after all my mistakes, mess ups, successes, and efforts, I have no judgment. Everyone is exactly as they should be, and the best part of that, is I get to see and experience new things through and with others. I try to take my expectations out of the equation to learn through, and with others on their individual and unique journey to support those that I care about.*

❖ ❖ ❖

Kathryn

Twenty two years old, living in a four-plex with four room mates, off campus (and we love it). In a charming area of a large city on the west coast with a wonderful view of the water, some of the building tops downtown, and on some clear days, the mountains. Our apartment not only spoils us in terms of the quality and space it provides, but it is also much cheaper than living on campus, which saves us all a little bit of money. One of the girls has been my roommate since freshman year of college. Although all of my roommates are either pre-med or nursing, I am studying graphic design and business marketing and will graduate in June with these two majors.

I am not married and I have no children. I have been in a serious relationship for three and a half years, and we plan on getting married in a little over a year. My boyfriend attends a University three hours from my school, so the phone bills are a bit of a shock every month. We are able to see each other a few times a month, on weekends, which makes the long distance seem a bit shorter.

I have had work experience in the graphic design field in an internship experience, but I am currently unemployed and looking for part-time work or other internship opportunities before I graduate. I plan on living on the west coast after graduation. Since I am a college student, but still supported a bit by my family at home, I would classify myself as middle class. I am Caucasian, with Irish, English, and Welsh blood in my family. I was raised in a non-denominational, Christian home, and continue to participate in church. I have been attending a University Church for three years. Politics do not interest me as much as they should, although I do hear some interesting political debates around the apartment in relation to health care. I have never campaigned for a candidate or been passionate about political issues. My policy is to not have much of an opinion unless I am fully educated in the topic, which explains my lack of political discussion.

I have been attending the University for the past four years, with the help of scholarships and grants. I was passionate about Marketing in high school, and had the opportunity to compete in Public Relations campaigns for national competition my junior and senior year. I attended public school until college as a participant in the 'Challenge' program (elementary and middle school), as well as honors classes in high school, graduating as Valedictorian of my senior class. I am graduating with two majors: Art and Business Marketing.

Did "right"— I have been motivated to succeed in areas of my life where I focus my energy. I have achieved scholastic achievement as well as been involved in the community and the church. I have sought advice and mentorship from various sources, whether personal friends, or professionals in the business world, which has helped me focus my goals and challenge my thinking.

Do "over"— Take more risks. I always want to have all my ducks in a row, which often leads me away from riskier alternatives. I haven't had many times in life where I have fallen hard and ultimately failed, because I have learned from the advice and experience of so many others. I wish I had taken more risks so I could have more experiences to draw back on. I still have time to do that though, so it is not something that I regret. That's what I am doing right now while I am looking for employment!

Question asked— I always love to hear the stories of older women and how they encountered difficulty in their lives and how they overcame that. Hearing advice from seasoned veterans has always been of interest to me. I would probably ask them, 'What are you most proud of in your life?' and 'What do you still want to change in your life that you haven't been able to tackle yet?

What would you tell— To tell women that are older than me: Please do not generalize all women (or men) of my generation as spoiled and disrespectful. Allow yourself to get to know women that are younger than you so you can appreciate what they go through on a daily basis – all the pressures of society and the expectations put on us. Appreciate people from my generation that are respectful, and compliment them on it.

To tell women that are younger than me: Continue to be respectful of those who are older than you. They deserve respect, even if they do not understand entirely what you are going through.

Travel: It teaches you more than you think. Allow yourself to be stretched in other cultures. You learn exponentially more in other countries than you do here – about the world, about others, and about yourself.

❖ ❖ ❖

Karrie

I am 23 years old. I live in an urban area with my 6 year old daughter. I am single and have never been married. I work part time and am also a full time student at a community college. I would definitely be termed as lower class. As far as race, I am mixed, although I would normally reply Alaska Native. I am not as involved in politics as I probably should be. I don't really watch television and I rarely pick up a newspaper so I am really out of touch with the world. I realize that politics are important and I should be more involved but when voting time comes around I usually ask family members which politicians to vote for. As far as education, I graduated from High School and enrolled at the state university and attended for a semester before transferring to a community college where I intend to graduate.

Did "right"— I feel like there are several things that I did right in my life. I would have to say that the first thing that comes to my mind is choosing to keep my daughter. I was 16 when I found out I was pregnant and 17 when she was born. Many girls in the same situation may have had an abortion but the thought never crossed my mind. To me it just wasn't an option. I was going to be a mother. She is the most wonderful child and I am truly blessed because of her. I cannot even begin to think about where I would be in life without her. She is my strength and inspiration to be a better person.

" Play is not the opposite of work. It is the attitude
with which we enjoy the company of others."
– *Roberta*

"Believe in yourself. The mind
is a powerful tool, use it
wisely. Spend as much time
listening as you do talking."
– *Kate*

For me to give her life was without doubt one of the choices I have made in life in which I know I did the right thing.

Do "over"— Since my father died when I was nine and my mother died when I was eighteen, I would like to live my live over starting as a young child. I would remember never to take life for granted. I would have clung to my mother and father every chance I had and let them know how much I loved them. I couldn't have saved my father but when he was nearing death, he asked whether I would like to spend more time with him, and I chose not to. I had no idea that he was dying because I only saw him once a year. My mother was an alcoholic. I knew she had a problem but I never realized that it was possible for her to die at such a young age. Sometimes we just do not realize how precious life is. I would have done anything to help her quit drinking. I cannot really explain the joy it would bring to me if I could live my childhood over. Even if the results were the same in the end, I would cherish the time I spent with my parents while it lasted.

Question asked— I would like to ask an older women, what should I do now to be successful later in life?

What would you tell— I would like to tell a younger women that life may seem like fun and games and then reality strikes. You never know what surprise life will bring you next. For me it was a daughter and she is so special, I would not trade her for the world. However, when we're young we seem to think that we are invincible but we aren't. I never thought that I would end up pregnant in high school, but I did. I don't want to sound cliché BUT… don't think it can't happen to you, because it happened to me.

❖ ❖ ❖

Nicole

I'm 23, I live on a farm on the edge of a city with two of my big brothers on our family farm. No children. Very much single. Finishing up a Masters and about to embark on the best job in the world... for me! As a Youth Minister. I guess I come from middle class, the farming world is pretty up and down so we didn't have very much while I was growing up but we were never in want. I was an intern for two years and now I'm a student so... I live off my brothers and a wee part time job! But yeah I'd say we're middle class status. I'm British. Christian. I have very little political interest, this is something that is changing as I grow older but I am thankful that there are people around me with enough passion and enthusiasm for politics that make up for my lack. I do seek to learn from them. Education, went right through school, I have a Bachelor of Theology and am working towards a Masters in Theology in Ministry and Mission.

Do "right"— I have loved. I have taken risks based on God's faithfulness... so really not so much of a risk!

Do "over"— I'd like to have listened to those who knew me best rather than a love that blinds. If there is a next time I'll know for sure then. It's good to realize the wrong, repenting, forgiving, pondering to see who I am and what I want, but there's no point in wasting time on regret... Wasting time on bitterness and sadness however seems often unavoidable. Other women, good friends have made me see that indeed "It'll be fine!"

Question asked— I would ask any age could you live/have lived without him?

What would you tell— I would tell any other woman you are not alone. You are not the only one. You are beautiful. Life hurts, but it is worth it. Grab every opportunity, but as you do pay attention to those you might be leaving behind. Love because you were first loved.

—TEN YEARS LATER—

I'm 33, 2 of my brothers still have our family farm but I've moved south to just outside the city. Very happily married, first baby on the way. Still doing "the best job in the world... for me," not the same job as 10 years ago though. Moved over a little, still working with the church but now a cluster of churches developing Family & Youth work, essentially helping the churches be helpful in their communities, getting to know families and young people and how the church can serve them, working with schools to build community links and develop their religious studies where appropriate and religious observance creatively. Still middle class but the lines are pretty blurred and enjoy working and relating through the ranges of class, age and background. Scottish. Christian. Slightly more political interest... but mostly in re-watching political shows on T.V., which doesn't do much for me attempting to vote here! Certainly more interested in local politicians who are keen to serve their communities. Education, I got that Masters and have found it very practical and useful. Ten years on I'd love to branch out a little with a study at home Master program in Children & Youth Studies. But paying the mortgage and providing for a wee one take precedence!

Reading back to ten years ago I see a lot of healing in the last 10 years, a lot has moved on but the core of faith, family and being helpful have stuck. I'm grateful as I think of my friends and supporters of those days and blessed that many are still the same, blessed to have picked up a few more along the way. Had I been able to tell myself then what life would be like in 10 years... I'd have thought it a dream not possible, but then as I have reaffirmed daily: God knows what you need. And it's pretty freakin awesome. Not easy! But awesome and beyond what I could have planned.

Do "right"— I've continued to trust and to love... and the risks keep coming!

Do "over"— Ha ha! Still trotting out "It'll be fine!" and "Mustn't

" My daughter is the most wonderful child and I am truly blessed
because of her. I cannot even begin to think about where I would
be in life without her. She is my strength and inspiration to be a
better person. For me to give her life was without doubt one of the
choices I have made in life in which I know I did the right thing."
–Karrie

" I've let myself cry even when
I thought it was stupid."
–Laura

grumble!" Much to the consternation of a counselor I saw for a while! The years of looking back sometimes shed a more honest light on regrets. I think if I could do over some things I'd stay stronger, truer... but then I think the journey has all contributed to who I am. Choosing who to listen to is an ongoing struggle for all of us, we do the best we can at the time, can't ask much more than that.

Question asked— Oh the angst of younger years! I'd just ask now, "What's your story?" To ask a narrower question misses opportunities to engage and learn things you didn't even know you could learn. It helps you keep out of your own head a bit.

What would you tell— Pretty much the same! I might add "Go on, give it a go!"

❖ ❖ ❖

Sherri

I am 24, single, childless, and Asian (Vietnamese). I have no interest in religion or politics on a personal level (I am not religious nor affiliate myself with a political party), although I enjoy discussing both. I am a college graduate from a university with BA degrees in English and Business. Economically, I am currently lower to middle class, although educationally I am middle to upper class. I am currently working as a Proofreader, although I will be attending graduate school for graphic design.

Did "right"— I made independence important in my life–in activities, choices, and viewpoints.

Do "over"— I would like to have adapted and dealt with situations more quickly. I respond to things appropriately, but I linger too long and am slow to move on.

Question asked— How do you maintain a separate identity in a marriage (especially with children)?

What would you tell— Learn what makes you happy as soon as you can. Also, balance is required but that doesn't necessarily mean that every aspect of your life should be given exactly equal amount of care. The ratio should reflect the varying amounts of happiness you derive from different things. (I think).

❖ ❖ ❖

Marsella

I'm 24 years old. I live in a western city with a roommate who is driving me nuts. I have no children (thank God). I am single, but have a serious boyfriend who is an officer in the Army. He is currently serving six months in Afghanistan. It has put a strain on our relationship.

I work for a controversial Republican Congressman. I plan all of his district special events as well as serving as his district business liaison. I would consider myself culturally upper middle class, but according to my income level, I am just above poverty. One of the perks of working for the House of Representatives is most certainly NOT the pay. I have a BA in business. I am white and Catholic. My faith plays a central role in my life. While I'm not hardcore, my faith is something that is very private and very comforting to me. No matter what happens in my life I can count on the quiet, peaceful tradition of the Catholic church. Even though I know it's not "cool" to be Catholic, it's really important to me. I am a conservative feminist. I don't think I need to push my views on other people and do not respect people who do. I know who I am and what is important to me.

Did "right"— The part of my life in which I have most excelled has been my career. I have worked very hard all my life. I hold my college's record for number of internships done while in attendance. I started working when I was 14, not because I needed to, but because I wanted to. I also pride myself on being a great friend.

Do "over"— I wish I could do over college. I feel like there were so many opportunities of which I could have taken advantage. I would have traveled more and interned for the government and taken more languages. I also would have double majored. AND, I would have dumped my college boyfriend the day I knew he wasn't the right person for me. I wasted time and effort.

Question asked— The question I would like to ask someone older is how they have reconciled their "pipe dreams" and reality. I'm just not ready to give up on being something enormously great. I don't think I should – but at some point, you have to look reality in the face and buy that house in the suburbs, right? Have they? If so, how can you do that? AND – what is the secret to success (minus the cheesey lines) – I want a clear and focused answer.

What would you tell— I would tell someone younger to not take things personally. Politics has really toughened me up, but it's made me stronger. Never be afraid to stand up for yourself. And start saving money. Today's culture is so focused on having designer handbags and shoes and all that. Read the *"Millionaire Next Door."* If you want to be truly wealthy, you just can't do all that! Not yet anyway! I don't mean to be a stick in the mud, but to be truly independently wealthy, you have to sacrifice a little sometimes.

❖ ❖ ❖

Diana

I am 26 and have been married for two and a half years and have known him for seven. I grew up in a small mountain town outside of a large western city. My parents are still together and I have one older sister whom I adore. Family is very important to me and it hurts me not to be near them. I currently live in a small mountain town outside of a city on the west coast and the only family I have is my dear husband and our two wonderful dogs. We are expecting our first child in four months and we are very excited to make a family and place for ourselves although we long to go home someday. My

husband's job brings us to a different part of the country and we
are enjoying exploring a new place. My husband is a mechanic and
brings home most of our money, however I am an admin at a larger
commercial Real Estate firm and I am learning tons every day, I
make a fair wage and between the two of us we manage to live nicely
within our modest lifestyle. Ideally I would like a home to raise
our children, but between the cost of living, health care, and the
future opportunities at my work we do not see that in our future. I
love my job and I have my real estate license so that I can learn the
business, however right now my job is focusing on marketing. I am
a very liberal democratic and I am very strong in my beliefs, my
husband kind of has to agree with me or I tell him how it is! I am a
practicing Catholic and my husband is Christian so we both attend
the Catholic church and plan to raise our children in the faith. I have
my BA from a University in Spanish and I have done nothing with
my language degree since the day I graduated, however I believe that
just having the degree helped me to get my current job.

Did "right"— I chose an active lifestyle. My parents are very active
and I learned to enjoy many activities. I chose to continue to have
a healthy lifestyle and have made that a large portion of who I am
today. I am very happy that I created that habit early on for I have
benefited from it throughout my life and I know that I will continue
to benefit from it in the future.

Do "over"— Many things. I would have liked to had more fun in
high school and college. I feel that my low self esteem and my
emphasis on education deterred me from really getting a bit wild
and enjoying some fun times, I feel that I did some catching up in
college, but then I married and it died away. I think that education
is really important but it really has not placed me anywhere that I
would not be if I had loosened up a bit. However on the other hand
I feel that I should have been more determined on my education and
realized that I could have studied anything I wanted to. I did not feel
that I had the intelligence to do some of the things I wanted so I just

went with what was easy. I should have thought it through a lot more and either taken time off and had some fun while I figured it out. I feel that my education was a waste and there are so many more things that I would have liked to pursue.

Question asked— I would not ask for advice, because who knows if I would listen (I have not in the past) I would not ask for her opinion, but I would ask her to tell me about her life and I would listen. I would want to hear about her husband, about her childhood, about her children, about her life adventures, and I would listen.

What would you tell— Younger woman is that she CAN do ANYTHING that she wants to, that to really pursue what she wants and to really find something that she enjoys no matter what it is no matter what the challenges are. That intelligence is not everything and appearance is not everything, but love and happiness are everything and that is what she needs to seek, something that she loves and makes her happy!

—TEN YEARS LATER—

To begin, I can admit that life is very different 10 years later. Reading through my notes about my life ten years ago makes me realize that I have gone through so many changes.

Not long after my original entry we did give birth to our first son. He was born in June. I took a three month maternity leave and then against my own desires returned to work shortly after. Work turned into a career and I began traveling frequently and working long hours. My husband worked four ten hour days and I had most Fridays off, so my son was in daycare for three days of the week. However, I would go to work before the sun rose and leave after sunset and I began to get very depressed. My son was an extremely colicky baby and the first six months were filled with sleepless nights and a crying child whom we loved and adored with every breath in our bodies. We both worked hard to maintain and we even got pregnant when our son was 1 ½.

One morning after breakfast, my husband drove into our driveway and accidently ran over and killed our family dog, the dog that we treated like a child before our son was born. This event brought out deep resonate feelings inside of me. I realized how short life was and how I did not want my children to grow up not knowing their grandparents like I did mine. My husband was very kind about my feelings and he did not argue. Although he loved the west coast so much, he agreed to move back to the mid-west to live near our friends and family. He had no idea how much the move would really change our lives.

My son was 2 and I was 7 months pregnant when we moved to where my parents resided. My husband started a paint company and worked for my father and I went back to school to get my masters and teaching license. I knew that I did not want my children in daycare during the summers and evenings and that I could use my Spanish if I were a teacher. We bought a house and gave birth to our second son. This baby was very happy and I was able to stay at home for his first two years of his life.

I started working as a substitute teacher when our children were two and four. I loved working again and being out among others, but we began to have problems at home, I felt like he did not work hard enough, and he became angry and very upset. He stopped talking to me, and we lost a connection that we once had. I tried to get him to see a therapist and offered that we go to couple therapy, but he did not believe in therapy and refused. I was not easy either, I expected him to work harder than he wanted, and I expected him to be someone else. I lost my love for him. His unkindness and unwillingness to meet new people and leave the house, and my ability and need to be a social butterfly drove us apart. I was craving a social life, I wanted friends with husbands and he just wanted to stay home. I left him. The kids and I moved in with my parents.

We got a divorce, during that time, life was wretched. I finished my masters and got a job teaching. I moved into a condo and committed all my time to my children. We moved on. My ex-husband fell in love again with a young woman and they have been living together for two years and hopefully will get married soon. We all get along well, that is not to say that we don't have our differences, but we are all adults and understand the need for stability and family for our children. Our sons love both sets of grandparents. Every time that they get back from visiting their grandparents out of the state, the kids tell me that they want to live there when they grow up!

The boys are incredibly well adjusted and happy. I am a middle school Spanish teacher and I love my job. I am starting school again this fall for my second masters, this one in teacher leadership. I am not in a relationship with anyone and have failed at every one I have tried since I was married.

I think my ex husband is much happier with his life now. He absolutely despised the expectations I held on him and now because of his girlfriend and her family money he has been able to quit his job and start his own business with his own hours, with no one telling him how hard to work. She is much more similar to him than I ever was and they are happy.

My parents have the boys every Friday night and they have an amazing connection with them. Because of my parents they have been able to go up to our cabin and form the same childhood memories that I have. They have been able to make relationships with their cousins and spend weekends with them. They have been able to go on adventure after adventure around the area because of my parents' generosity and willingness to explore. Additionally, at every soccer game, class play, or any event, my kids are surrounded with love and family by myself, my parents, and their father.

As I read through my comments from many years ago, I realized how full of life I was, I had not been disappointed by life yet and held such a breath of eagerness and happiness. I tasted a bit of the depression that was about to take over my life, but I still have that youthful set of mind.

I was surprised that I had written about my active lifestyle. That is one thing that remains constant. I am currently training for a triathlon and

" Wasting time on bitterness and
sadness however seems often
unavoidable. Other women, good
friends have made me see that
indeed 'It'll be fine!'"

–Nicole

" I do know that I've been a good person. I'm a good friend, a good
daughter. I try to listen. I try to point out the positives in people.
I have love to spare, which often causes me great pain."

–Laura

been active throughout my life, it is my rock that I rely on to get me through tough times and help keep my mind straight.

Lastly, I cannot believe that I actually said that I would not ask for any advice! Advice is what I absolutely needed, I wish someone would have told me that my marriage could be saved if I just let me husband be who he was and be okay with that and just work on my own career.

So now I want advice. How do I survive? How do I make sure that my kids are all right and they will not make the same mistakes that I did? That they have fun in school and have a good balance that they do not crave it when they are an adult and starting a family? I want them to be passionate about life and learning and to take it seriously so that they can have a career they love and make money so they are not struggling like me. Can anyone give me some advice on how to do this and how to keep going every day?

❖ ❖ ❖

Kate

I am 29 years old and currently live in Europe because of work, though soon will be moving back to the suburbs on the east coast. I am recently married (6 months the end of April), but my husband and I are apart (only for a few more months) because of our respective jobs and responsibilities. We are lower/middle class and don't have children yet, but are looking forward to being blessed with them in the next few years. I am a true reflection of the American melting pot with some Western European, Chilean, and Palestinian running through my veins. I am definitely a Democrat, though every-so-often the Republican point of view shows through. I went to school in the mid-west and have my BA in Political Science and Communication. I am also part way through my Master's Degree.

Did "right"— Followed my dreams. People have often thought I was crazy or rash for making some of the career and life choices I've made, but I've always followed my dreams.

Do "over"— I wish I would have listened more as a child/student. It wasn't until I was older that I really understood all that people had to give. I wish I would have paid more attention and learned more at a younger age.

Question asked— How do you cope with the unknown? What advice would you give to younger women on how to not let the unknown cloud today's happiness?

What would you tell— Believe in yourself. The mind is a powerful tool, use it wisely. Spend as much time listening as you do talking.

❖ ❖ ❖

in my 30's

" I'd like to tell her that most of us are struggling with one thing or another, and we could probably stand to share more of that with the people around us, so maybe everyone wouldn't feel quite so alone."

–Laura

Susan

I am 30 years old and live in a suburb of a large western city. I have
no children, but have two cats. I work in higher education
as an Internship Coordinator for a University. My husband and I
are in what I would consider the upper-middle class of society
based on household income, professions and life style. I am African-
American, but have a combination of Italian-American,
Native-American, Mongolian, German and English in my family
history. My husband and I are in that age group that is still searching
for the perfect religion, but were raised Lutherans (Christians). My
political interests side mostly with the democratic party, but some of
my views are becoming a bit more conservative, just depends what
the issue is.

Did "right"— I feel what I did right in my life includes: marrying
my husband (9 years in August), moving from mid-west to west
coast (the wild west for 4 years and running), embracing my creative
and analytical natures, waiting to become a mom (waiting until my
mid 30's), getting a higher education (BA in Art History, MA in Arts
Administration, and a Web Design certification), finding a love for
playing the violin, dance and the great outdoors.

Do "over"— What I'd like to do over in my life includes: at times
my career choices, not moving out west sooner, not committing to
exercise and a work-life balance more.

Question asked— I'd like to ask women my age: if they find it
difficult to balance career choices with motherhood choices, find it
difficult to succeed as well as men in career choices, if they find it
difficult to balance health with work, find it difficult to create new
support groups when moving from their home state, have any advice
for getting your husband to respect you as much as they
do their mothers and establishing yourself as a the matriarch of your
nuclear family.

What would you tell— I would tell a younger women: don't rush to
find the perfect husband or career – give yourself time to explore

and to know yourself first. I would tell an older woman: give younger women more respect and empathy for the new challenges we face dealing with career and motherhood. I would tell a woman my age: be proud, find inspiration in everything you do, give back to those younger than you, and learn from the lessons and mistakes of our elders.

—TEN YEARS LATER—

I relocated from the west coast to the mid-west in 2007 and have resided in the same state for the last six years. During this time I received my doctorate in Higher Education and have had the opportunity to research and teach at the University. I am currently serving as the Associate Director of Graduate Admissions. I am no longer married, I actually divorced my husband in 2005. However, the happy side of life is that I am engaged to a new brilliant and beautiful man who shares my passion for life as a scholar in a university setting. My social class would be considered upper-middle class based upon my occupation and education; however, with the debt load of student loans, I live a lower-middle class life style. I would still describe myself as an African American heterosexual woman who is an interdisciplinary, intersectional and interfaith scholar-practitioner whose research is rooted in issues of diversity and higher learning, equity and access, inclusion and radical humanism to provide a reclaiming process for non-white communities to document their experiences in predominantly white built campus environments.

Did "right"— *I feel that I was too young (21 years old) to get married the first time and that this ultimately resulted in my marriage ending at age 31. Being married in my 20's was a time for my own self-discovery, growth and development. While I was considering becoming a mother during the time I initially responded, I have found great joy in finding myself first as a woman, now as a scholar and recently becoming an Aunt to my younger sister's daughter. I still hold a deep passion for music, dance, painting, poetry and writing; however, the* *focus of this passion has become more enriched by learning about and embracing the roots and history of my cultural heritage as an African American women. I am now in the transformation process of become holistically whole (culturally, spiritually, physically, intellectually, etc).*

Do "over"— *I would have liked to pursue my doctorate 10 years ago, but I am happy that this dream always stayed with me and I am looking forward to more doors opening because of the choice that I made to pursue my higher degree. In fact, I just received a book contract to publish my dissertation through a university press and had the opportunity to publish my first article on my dissertation last year. I feel like I am "finally" on the right path, career wise and personal life wise. However, I am still seeking a stronger commitment to exercise and a work-life balance. Although, I have found deeper balance and peace through a sitting meditation practice.*

Question asked— *Nearing the age of 40, I would change my question to: How do you find time every day to give back to yourself, make peace with yourself and to love yourself so that you can give to those in your life and in the community?*

What would you tell— *I would stand by everything that I stated, remarkably! Yet, would add that the true way to happiness, peace and real love, begins with yourself. Love yourself, every imperfect part of you, see life as a journey – not a goal line and listen/see/feel the beauty and miracles that surround you to keep you going when times get tough as well as during those celebratory moments.*

❖ ❖ ❖

Liz

I am 31 years old, I live in a large city on the west coast in a neighborhood with three other ladies in their late 20's and early 30's. I am single, no children at this point. I am an administrative assistant and looking to go to grad school next fall for school counseling. I'm used to being in the middle class, but in reality

I'm in more of the lower economic bracket. I am Caucasian and a Christian. I tend to be split between Republicans and Democrats... I think we need a balance. I have a bachelor's in Christian Education.

Did "right"— I have some great long-term friends that I am thankful to have. I have traveled and worked/lived in Europe, so those are things that I am glad that I have done. I'm a godmother for my friends' little boy and that makes me happy.

Do "over"— Commit more quickly to people and friendships, but really I'm not sure that would change since it's more my personality to take my time in commitments.

Question asked— How do you maintain a young playful heart as responsibilities grow in your life?

What would you tell— Don't hold grudges, get past how you feel about things and find out the facts – it saves a lot of time to get to the truth quickly and past what you perceive to be true. Spend time with the Lord and let him ground you (so many things will tug you in different directions, you need to know who you are apart from all those things). If you worry, stop worrying, it has never turned out to be helpful. Give yourself and other people as many second chances as needed – but stand up for yourself too.

❖ ❖ ❖

Laura

I am 33. I live in a suburb on the east coast. I love my state, although I hate the traffic. I live alone, although my parents, my sister, grandmothers and extended family of aunts, uncles and cousins are mostly nearby.

I have no children, which is currently a source of great disturbance for me, but I'm trying to deal with it without panicking. I'm single, unhappily so, but I've just split for good from my ex-boyfriend who was merely my "best friend" for the past two years. I work in higher education as an administrator now, and have a master's degree, so I guess you'd say I'm middle class. I'm in a lot of debt from school loans and bad choices in college, so money is a sticky wicket as well. I am a registered Democrat with independent leanings. I am completely opposed to the Iraq war, and to just about everything our President has ever done since the day he was inflicted upon the planet. I have very frightening feelings about the political system in this country, but I haven't gotten involved, which isn't good. I spend most of my time trying to keep my head above water lately... job, friends, dealing with intermittent depression... Sometimes life feels very heavy. I was raised Catholic but don't practice, although I'm not as opposed to the Church as many of us who lapsed. I'm white, typical Irish/German background. This sounds a bit depressing, this synopsis, but I'm a lot more than this... just going through a bit of a rough patch right now! I love music. I love to write. I love to read. I love the movies and concerts. I love my dog so much it hurts. I love the beach and think I'll probably live by the ocean someday.

Did "right"— Sometimes I feel like, "not much," but I do know that I've been a good person. I'm a good friend, a good daughter. I try to listen. I try to point out the positives in people. I have love to spare, which often causes me great pain, but I hear that's typical.

I've been funny often times when I could have chosen to be mean or silent. I've traveled some but not enough. I've maintained good relationships with my parents in spite of some disagreements that could have caused major rifts. I've focused on the importance of the bonds. I've forgiven people and hoped that they would forgive me. I've apologized when I know I've behaved badly.

I was born with a cleft lip and palate and struggled with my weight for 20 years. I've not let either be an excuse for hiding from the world or from other people. I've tried to solve problems.

I've struggled with depression and have been honest about that too. I'm not ashamed of it. I don't blare it from the mountaintop, but if I think it'll help someone, I share.

I have been honest with the men I've been involved with, sometimes to a fault. Sometimes it doesn't always make me look good, but at least I have a clear conscience.

I've let myself cry even when I thought it was stupid.

I followed my heart to the mid-west for someone I thought I would marry. I was entirely wrong about that, but at least I'll never wonder what may have happened, and I made some good friends and learned a tad of independence.

I have been fearless in my career, in one way. I've never been afraid to quit a job that was making me miserable. I may not know what the right thing is, but I sure as hell know the wrong thing when it's going down. I've tried a variety of fields that speak to my strengths – media, counseling, nonprofit education, higher ed admin... I still don't know which one will be the charm, but I'm not wedded to any particular path. Sometimes I wish I were but I have come to accept that this is just not how I'm wired.

Do "over"— My freshman year of college, which I think was a real turning point for me. I nearly failed out and set myself up in a pattern, which led me not to complete the degree in journalism that I sought.

My relationship with my last boyfriend. I still have deep feelings for him that are very difficult to get over. I wish I had gotten help for some of the emotional struggles that impacted my behavior at some critical points in the relationship. It might not have changed the outcome but it would have made the experience better for both of us, I think.

I would love to go back to childhood and have someone put musical instruments in my hand so I could have learned to play the piano, guitar, even drums! Early on.

" Be proud, find inspiration in everything
you do, give back to those younger than
you, and learn lessons and mistakes
from our elders."
  –Susan

" Even if the results were the same in the
end, I would cherish the time I spent with
my parents while it lasted."
  –Karrie

I hate to say I'd do anything over because I'd have to trade something of value for most of it... stuff I wouldn't have gotten if I'd done something different.

I do know I'd do over my financial situation. I would have forced myself to be wiser about money early on, and I wouldn't have borrowed so much for school. It can really haunt you later in life, during years when you really need to get things accomplished.

Question asked— Do you feel like a sham sometimes at work? Are you all as goal-oriented as you seem or when you shut your door is e-mail sometimes all that you can handle?

Do you feel secure as a single person?

What would you tell— I'd like to tell her that most of us are struggling with one thing or another, and we could probably stand to share more of that with the people around us so maybe everyone wouldn't feel quite so alone.

I'd like to tell her that we live in strange times, where the expectations are cloudy and the demands are intense. It's okay to feel pissed off about that... but hopefully you'll find the support you need to have a decent life in spite of the confusion.

❖ ❖ ❖

Adrian

I am 36 years old. I live within the city limits of a large city, but it feels quite suburban. I live with my husband of 14 years and my 7 year old son. I worked at a large university for six years after college, then became a stay-at-home mom, but I never stay home. I am middle class, with my husband's job paying quite respectably. But, we both believe in living below our means, so as my husband's income has gone up, we've raised our standard of living a little, but for the most part, we save. We're saving for retirement with no belief in the government to ever give us anything back. We're saving for what we've been calling The Big Trip. But we're not sure where that is yet: New York City, Washington DC or perhaps Europe. I am white. But, I've never liked that title. I feel more peachy/pink. And I have a strong heart to improve race relations in the U.S. Especially between blacks and whites.

I am a Christian and take my faith very seriously. I study the Bible and I'm now working on a committee to set up Bible studies all over the region after a large Revival in my city.

I can hardly stand politics. I am neither Republican nor Democrat. I don't understand the whole gun rights thing – seems to me that such tools of violence should be made extremely difficult to get our hands onto. I am pro-life. But, I'm also pro-social programs. So I have things about the Democrats I agree with and things about the Republicans that I agree with, but neither one do I agree with completely.

I have a four-year degree in Psychology. I have a great respect for my education and want everyone to get a good education. Even though I don't have a paying job, I use my education daily.

Did "right"— I went to college and got a good education. In raising my son I insisted that the TV be put inside a stand that has doors that cover over the TV. Out of sight, out of mind. I'm not against TV, just that limiting it has been a really good thing for our family. About the time that I got a TV stand with doors, I started taking our then 18 month old son to the library every week. It's made a big difference. We watch very little TV. In fact, there aren't any TV shows that we watch. But, we love movies that we check out from the library or rent from our local video store.

Do "over"— I would save my virginity until marriage. I didn't, and I regret it, greatly.

" Have any advice for
getting your husband to
respect you as much as
they do their mothers and
establishing yourself as
the matriarch of your
nuclear family."

–Susan

Question asked— Younger woman with preschool children: How do you manage having so many roles, full-time childcare, wife, homemaker, possibly even outside-the-home career? (I had a really tough time during that stage of my son's life).

Older woman over 70: What has kept your relationship good with your son(s) and or daughter(s)? And what do you do, if you discover that you don't really like the person that your child is choosing to marry?

Any woman who has been there: How do you handle critical people?

What would you tell— John 3:16, "For God so loved the world that he gave his only begotten son that whosoever should believe in Him shall not perish but have everlasting life."

—TEN YEARS LATER—

Health changes!

My son was diagnosed with Autism Spectrum Disorder (ASD) specifically Pervasive Developmental Delay – Not Otherwise Specified (PDD-NOS). My son was 10 years old when diagnosed and it took me more than a year to accept the diagnosis. Just the title of it "Not Otherwise Specified" seemed to me like a clarification phrase something like this: "He kind-of has autism, sorta, but not really." When I could see how much my son was suffering in school by bullies and honestly just regular kids who didn't understand him, I decided to homeschool him for middle school (6-8) grades. Yet, when I asked my son if he would like to homeschool for 6th grade, he quickly replied, "NO Mom! 5th grade!" So I knew right there that he was done with his elementary school; a K-5 school. In the end, we homeschooled four years, (5-8) grades. Then my son said he wanted to go to high school. He is now a junior in high school and thriving.

My husband was diagnosed with multiple sclerosis at the age of 39. This diagnosis was made on the basis of MRI's and presenting symptoms of tingling scalp, arms and legs. This diagnosis also took me awhile to absorb. I had always heard that MS was difficult to diagnose and supposedly took years of unexplained symptoms to come to a vague conclusion of MS. But, with changing medical advancements the diagnosis was made quickly. At first my husband only had odd sensations and very little in terms of noticeable symptoms. But 7 years later his walking is greatly effected. He typically uses a cane. His ability to walk any distance is greatly reduced. We now have a handicap placard for the car. Our lives are now changing on a daily basis. Sometimes my husband has enough energy to do ordinary daily tasks and often he doesn't. It has changed household duties, vacation plans, and especially interactions with our son. "Dad, simply can't do the things he used to."

Did "right"—Make "house" rules and "family" rules. I've set up rules for my son bracketed with the concept on what we choose to do in our family or in our house. Such that in our house we don't play rated M video games. But, if he goes to a friend's house, I have no control over what he plays there. So, I've set the rules up in such a way that he can see what we've chosen and he's expected to make his own choices when away from home. My hope is that I'm setting him up for future choices with a solid background of knowledge on our choices and the reasons behind them.

As a family we watch TV and movies together. This offers us the opportunity to discuss what we see and also to know what our son is watching at least in our house.

We read books aloud together as a family.

Apologize! I try to always apologize to my son if I think I've done wrong. I'm NOT perfect and I don't believe I have a good excuse just because "I'm the mom."

Deal with your own baggage. I have my own issues of depression and obsessive-compulsive disorder. My growing up years was tough with a *chaotic environment. I'm dealing with it. I've sought counseling and reconciliation with family. I'm dealing with my own problems; not allowing the past to fester in the present thereby fouling the future.*

Question asked*—Questions I'd ask an older person: What advice would you give about the fledging years? My son will be launching into the world on his own, soon. How have you handled illness in your family?*

❖ ❖ ❖

Marcia

I'm a 36 year-old Caucasian Hispanic Catholic, that currently resides in a very large mid-west city in an upper-middle class neighborhood with my husband and one dog. I have a Master's Degree in Business Management and am currently working on establishing the base for an animal welfare foundation I'm starting along with two other parties. Prior to doing my own thing, I was successful in marketing and product development. I do not pledge allegiance to either political party, but vote based on individual records and issues.

Did "right"*—* I got a good education.

Do "over"*—* I never would have married my first husband. Great guy, just not the "forever" guy for me.

Question asked*—* What is the one thing you would change in America?

What would you tell*—* If you want to find the "perfect" man for you, just be yourself, smile, laugh, and get his number. Never ditch your friends for a guy you meet when you are out with them. It sends the message that you are available until something better comes along. Don't go looking for love, it will find you.

❖ ❖ ❖

Lynn

I am 39 years old, white-college graduate. I am currently living with my husband in a suburb of a large city on the west coast for the past 14 years. I think of myself as a Lutheran, but my husband is a Presbyterian, we attend a Presbyterian Church. We are upper-middle class. I am a sales executive for a Fortune 500 pharmaceutical company. My husband is self-employed. We are a married couple without children.

Did "right"— I got a college degree because none of the doors would have been opened to me had I not finished college. I think I've been goal orientated, visualized and made those goals happen. Good at persevering despite setbacks. I've been good about not allowing a chronic illness to side step me from my dreams. I have done a good job turning a bad situation into a positive one. Taking the adage that all these things turn into a long-term benefit. Christ is grooming me for something better.

Do "over"— I wish I would have been more in tune with the person I am now when I was younger. I think alcohol and drugs really side-tracked me as a person. I wish I was more in touch with myself as a teen. I would have gone into environmental law. Had I not anesthetized myself so much... I would have made different decisions. I was too wrapped up in other people's opinions. I wish I had followed my dreams... I spent a lot of times pleasing my parents.

Question asked— I would like to ask an older women who did not have children, does she regret not having children or adopting?

What would you tell— In business never let them see you cry, because no one likes vulnerable people in the business world. Be careful who you trust because someone is out to get your job... you can be replaced. Also, women who do not have kids, start trying in your early 30's–it may take a long time. "Don't put on hold the things that you ultimately want... it may be too late."

—TEN YEARS LATER—

My place in life is exactly the same as it was 10 years ago. I am in a similar position with a different company, however, the job is pretty much the same. What has changed is that I have a new appreciation for life and for every day that God gives me on earth.

My original comments are great and I do not think that I would change any of them.

❖ ❖ ❖

in my 40's

" Getting a degree was essential to helping me think critically and become more interested in the world I live in rather than simply the world around me."

–Kameron

Mary

I am 40 years old. I live in a suburban area in the heart of the mid-west with my husband of 20 years and our two children, 9 and 3. I am white and I would put my economic position as lower/middle class but we "pretend" to be middle/upper class. I am an administrator for a surgical education program at a large University. I completed roughly two years of college but did not earn a degree. I have developed more interest in politics as I have gotten older. My husband is a Democrat all the way – I lean more towards the Republicans but I listen to what they have to say more than what they are.

Did "right"— I waited until I was older to have my children.

Do "over"— I would finish college and do something I truly like.

Question asked— Is it true that when your kids are ready to leave home, you are ready for them to leave and make their own life?

What would you tell— I believe that you are as young as your mind. Keep it active and keep in touch with the "younger" generation.

❖ ❖ ❖

Rita

I am 42, white, upper middle income, no political preference, three children 13, 11, 5.

Did "right"— Being honest.

Do "over"— Being so promiscuous, flirty?

Question asked— How do you deal with controlling people? How do you adjust to your husband's family when you have been raised so differently?

What would you tell— To relax. Life is too short. Enjoy kids, husband life.... Your children will survive.

❖ ❖ ❖

Kylie

I'm 42 years old, and live in a medium-size metropolitan area
(the city) with my husband of 18 years, along with my 18 year old
daughter, and 15 year old son. I work at home as a graphic designer
along with being an adjunct professor at two local Universities.
I have a strong faith in God, I belong to a large Presbyterian
Church and am very active within the congregation. Politically
I would consider myself divided between both the Democratic
and Republican parties, I believe very much in the social and
humanitarian efforts of the Democratic party, while valuing the
moral, religious and family issues of the Republican party. Currently
my vote is going more towards the Democratic, I feel the current
Republican candidate is too self-serving and has forgotten he is a
civil servant. I have always considered myself upper-middle class,
but my pocket book currently states that I am of lower economics…
as they say "house rich, but cash poor." My race is Caucasian, and I
have a graduate degree.

Did "right"— I prioritized my family… especially now that my
daughter is going away to college I feel good that I have spent a lot
of time with my kids. This has been a huge struggle since I have
worked full-time throughout their lives. I have chosen jobs that have
allowed me to stay home… I have searched out employment that
allowed me to have more control over the variables of time. This was
a huge endeavor when they were younger and it has really paid off
now. Unfortunately I did not watch my finances closer in order to
even out the low times… so the result of this effort has been great for
raising kids but not so great financially.

I have spent a lot of time in prayer and with a church community.

Over the years I look at my rewards from my church and it is
amazing, I have been an Elder, I have gone on mission trips,
I have close relationships with Pastors, I have great support
systems and people to call out to for prayer and I have learned

that I too am a great support. I have learned spiritual gifts and how to prioritize God.

Going back and getting my graduate degree... this was a huge undertaking–I was working full-time and my kids were young (honestly I don't know how I did it), but the rewards of self-esteem and identity have far out-weighed the effort. I would really encourage every mother to go back and re-educate themselves in their middle years. This process keeps you from wondering what you should be doing, because it helps you to focus on yourself at a time when all the focus is on your family. Funny thing is I found that my kids and I did a lot of homework together and it made me re-balance our schedule around all of our schoolwork.

Have a lot of family fun... we took a lot of family vacations when the kids were little and we had a lot of fun. When the years of money were flowing we took bigger trips, but even when we had none we always went camping! Really important, you don't get those years back!

Took a class on developing a personal mission statement... this has been a real gift, because it helps me say yes or no to the areas I involve myself with. If you are a giving person you will want to give to everything, but there is nothing left for you and your family so this statement has allowed me to evaluate my efforts. It is funny over the years I would have thought it would have changed meaning, but it is general enough that it has carried me through the past 10 years.

Do "over"— Money! I would have never opened up a credit card and been more diligent with my investments!!!

—I would like to have looked for mentors in my life, I think that is one area younger women have been wiser about.

—Seeking out healthy people—I wish I had spent more time looking at whether or not the people in my life were healthy for me.

—High School, I regret that so much of my focus was on popularity and not on my interests. I would have loved to have stuck with some of the clubs I started with, but quit because they were not "cool."

—Not focusing in on one area and becoming really good at it.

Question asked— If you have been successful in your career, what areas of your life did you have to let go of, and do you ever regret that, or have the results outweighed the consequences?

What would you tell— Spend time with God, bible study, fellowship and worship. Life is really hard, but through the grace of God you will find true joy and move through your days with value and purpose, and in the end you will have the richest of inheritances! Life changes so rapidly one minute you will be rich and then you are lacking, you will have many friends and then they will move, you will be the best at your job and then it turns, you will feel strong and healthy and then you get an illness, you will be a dedicated mom and then they grow up, and just as it turns sour and you want to scream hold on because the flowers bloom again! I have learned that the one thing that is constant is God's love for us, remember you are simply a sheep resting in His pasture. This is one area of your life you will never regret!

—TEN YEARS LATER—

A pivotal turn for me was when I turned 50. I am now 52 and I have to say I love this age. I don't like that my bones hurt a bit. But in fact I feel healthier and stronger than ever. I finally love myself enough to care for myself, both physically and spiritually. When I reflect on who I was I don't think I put enough emphasis on my physical care. It also makes a huge difference once your kids are raised. I have learned you will always worry about your kids and they are always at the top of my prayer chart, but the physical aspect of raising younger kids can be very draining, from physical early toddler years to all the school and sporting activities. One thing I have done in the past year is seek out

" I would really encourage every mother
to go back and re-educate themselves in
their middle years. This process keeps you
from wondering what you should be doing,
because it helps you to focus on yourself at
a time when all the focus is on your family."
–Kylie

" I believe that you are as young as your
mind. Keep it active and keep in touch
with the 'younger' generation."
–Mary

counseling. I cannot emphasize that enough. When I think about the struggles I have gone through I realize that most of the time I tried to solve them on my own rather than seeking out professional help. I have learned so many tools from my counselor. One of the most valuable tools for me has been writing my own narrative, that I am the maker of my story. I can choose to see things from a positive point of view or seek out the negative narrative for my life. This has been a big part of retraining my thoughts.

I think the biggest thing for me is the realization that life can take so many dramatic turns. In the last 10 years there has been a major recession, the mortgage crisis, a continuing war, natural disasters and increase in cancer. All of these things can flat line anyone. I have lost my house, my savings, and gained regrets I had no idea that could be so paralyzing. But I have also learned that life goes on and you have choices as to how you are going to move forward and engage in the process of living. It is a fight, it is a struggle, but it is also good, pure and beautiful. There are rhythms of life that we can't help but love, the sun rising, snow topped mountains, and the birth of a new baby. These are the rhythms that keep us going forward, these are the signs of love that keep us pressing on.

Because of the events of the past 10 years I don't plan as much anymore, I try to live more fully in the day, taking what it is that God is choosing for the script of my life. I am learning that HE provides all my needs, whether it is the presence of a friend, the excitement of travel, the rest of illness, the depth of pain of loss, or the coolness of diving into a deep-water lake. All of these things are HIS to give to me. I have learned not to shy away from my feelings, and that feelings are neutral as long as I am aware of them I can then choose how to react or act from them. I am also still learning not to give my power away. In the past I had a tendency to attract sarcastic, un-affirming friends that are still part of my life today. I am trying with God's grace not to give myself over to their verbal abuse, and to set limits as to how long I can be surrounded by their toxic presence. I think I have also learned that life does not have a graduation date, that we are continuing to grow, perhaps needing to be on a diet forever, needing to adjust our work out schedule, seek counseling through friends and professionals, to be intentional about our work flow and continually readjust. I think this type of flexibility helps us or at least me weather the ups and downs of life's climate. I guess if I were to walk back into the shoes of my 42 year old self I would say, don't be so afraid to make a mistake, it will happen no matter what, in ways that you had no idea. That is just the nature of life. And trust that as long as we live through Christ's lense the journey will be good.

Changes I would have made would be to seek more outside perspective. I think about the routes I have chosen and most of them were through the lense of my family systems. I would have looked at how other cultures perceived things such as health, family bonding, work, religion, finances and the skills we need to live a joyous life. Just saying this makes me realize how much I need to seek out new perspectives. This thought makes me excited about the next ten years.

❖ ❖ ❖

Kalyn
I am white, 42, suburban, three daughters: 14, 11, 5 and middle class. I am not religious and have no strong political believes. I have strong morals, Education MA and have an on-going career as a Speech Language Pathologist

Did "right"— Marrying my husband and having kids. Finishing my college degree.

Do "over"— Write more thank you notes. Emphasize the importance of thank you's... not only verbally but writing thank you notes... Acknowledge what other people do for you.

Question asked—

What would you tell— As a mother I would tell my daughters how beautiful, strong they are and that falling in love is very important in life. Also, that it is very important in life to have good girlfriends. That you can get through any crisis with good girlfriends. Girlfriends are different than a husband, mother and children even though I talk with my mother and husband and children every day.

—TEN YEARS LATER—

I am still alive! I am still married. I still have a job. My children are growing up. Last time I reported they were 14, 11 and 5. Now they are 23, 21 and 15! It is fun experiencing adult life with my older girls and I am happy I still have the youngest at home, which keeps me grounded.

I have a new daughter that we never knew about, a son-in law and 4 grandchildren. That has been a change in 10 years. I continue to work and love what I do. I know I am blessed for that. I am 10 years older. Health is still for the most part good but I really need to take care of myself both physically and mentally.

Did "right"— Still marrying my husband. Having kids and pursing a great career. Being connected with my family and friends.

Do "over"— Improving on my thank you notes but could still do better. Saying "thank you" is just two simple words. Save more money and plan more for the future. Didn't really have any idea how expensive college would be. Spend more time on vacation with my family.

Question asked— Does it ever get any easier?? Life, bills, marriage, etc.

What would you tell— I would tell my children they are the best thing in my (our) life. That their dad and I did one thing well, and that THEY are it! I have learned from my children and now they give me advice. I wish to live close to them, shop with them, have dinner with them and watch their children grow someday.

❖ ❖ ❖

Colleen

I'm 42 and live in the suburbs, I live with my partner and part time with her boys, 14 & 8. I'm technically unmarried. I'm a professional and consider myself middle class.

Did "right"— I got a college education.

Do "over"— I would have done better in school, and gotten a Masters Degree right after college.

Question asked— I would ask an older woman if they were 42 again, what would they do?

What would you tell— I would tell a younger woman to get as much school as possible and travel before they settle into a job or relationship and kids.

❖ ❖ ❖

Kameron

I am 43 years old, live in the suburbs of a western city with my husband of 10 years and my 4 1/2 year old daughter who was adopted by us at age one and is originally from China. I'm an attorney and consider my family to be middle class, though we are probably considered to be upper middle class. I am Caucasian, was raised Catholic though I only recently began attending church again. I have a bachelors and masters degree, both in social work, and a J.D. (law degree).

Did "right"— There are many things I think I did "right" in my life. Probably the most important was getting an education. At age 18, I had NO desire to go to college and wasn't real sure what I would do with my life. But in my family (both parents had HS educations, no college), it was NOT an option to not go to college. I'm thankful I did because of the people I met and the environment, which allowed me to experience things I had never before experienced and to think in a more academic manner about all kinds of things.

Getting a degree was critical to helping me think critically and become more interested in the world I live in rather than simply the world around me. It's also given me a tremendous amount of economic freedom in that I can change jobs at will and supports my family and myself if it were necessary. Having options in life is fundamental to my happiness.

Do "over"— I was raised to be and think very independently and that makes me somewhat difficult to get along with at times. It's taken me until my 40's to realize that depending upon others are actually a GOOD thing. I would be more open to being vulnerable to others, particularly men. That being said, and I know it sounds mutually inconsistent, the one thing I would have changed in my life was my indelible perception that in order to be "whole" I had to be married. I married relatively young and was quickly divorced which no one should have to go through. But I always felt like I had to meet a husband. My current husband is fabulous and I am happily married; I just wish I had felt better about being single and enjoyed that experience more at the time.

Question asked— Younger: Do you feel like we live in a "good" world and, if so, what helps you feel that way? What did your parents do that helped you develop some of your better qualities?

My age or older: How do you keep from worrying all the time about your own health/mortality and the health and happiness of your children? What have you done to raise children who are decent human beings who care about themselves and others?

—TEN YEARS LATER—

Very little has outwardly changed, yet so much has actually changed. Outwardly, I have more-or-less the same friends, my family remains healthy (although older and my father-in-law passed away about 9 years ago). We live in the same house and both myself and my

" I was raised to be and think very independently and that makes me somewhat difficult to get along with at times. It's taken me until my 40's to realize that depending upon others is actually a GOOD thing."

–*Kameron*

" It is very important in life to have good girlfriends. That you can get through any crisis with good girlfriends."

–*Kalyn*

husband work in the same fields as we did 10 years ago. On the other hand, 10 years is such a long time, although it seemed to have passed in the blink of any eye. My daughter continues to grow and mature and is now almost 14 years old. We have spent the past ten years focusing a lot on helping her achieve what we consider to be a healthy and well-balanced life and to that end, much of our day-to-day activities are those that are centered on her – homework, piano lessons, sporting activities, vacations. We had a simple yet fulfilling life 10 years ago and feel the same about our life today.

One of the things that really stands out about my comments ten years ago is my belief that obtaining an education is one of the things I "did right." This past year I left a position as an attorney with the government, which I held for 19 years and ventured out into a solo private practice. Every single day I smile and think about how fortunate I am, how thankful I am, that I have the education and training to be able to have so much freedom in my work life. I guess my thoughts on what I've "done right" really haven't changed at all. I also would ask the exact same questions today that I asked 10 years ago to someone younger or the same age. Those questions seem very personal and values-based and I guess you can say that really hasn't changed much for me over the years.

❖ ❖ ❖

Penny

I am 44 years old and live in a semi-urban west coast neighborhood, not the asphalt jungle of NYC, but definitely city! At this time I live alone, although I have lived with housemates in the past. No children. I worked as a photojournalist for most of my career primarily at city TV stations. I am now a trainer of software for an equipment manufacturer, so I go to TV stations and teach employees how to use newsroom software for editing and playing video to air.

I would say that I'm middle class comfortable. Caucasian, Protestant, fairly liberal politically and I have a masters degree in Broadcast Journalism.

Did "right"— I have taken risks moved around (sometimes by choice and sometimes forced). I followed my career dream to work behind a camera. I have put my weight on the Lord as a Christian believer and tried to center what I do on that values system. I have tried to love people with any risk that entails, although I have been challenged lately in my romantic life to move deeper than I have before.

Do "over"— Not too much, but I probably would have stuck things out in rowing until I made an Olympic team. I was too intent on getting a start on grad school and career and there was plenty of time for that. I was close to making a national team and could have easily stuck around longer.

Question asked— How have you dealt with disappointment? What have been your greatest joys apart from having children?

What would you tell— Be sure to take time in your 20's to explore— don't think that getting into a career track is the great mission. Travel, live somewhere other than the US! Keep playing at things.

❖ ❖ ❖

Pam

I am 46 years old. I have three children ages' 18, 16, and 11. My husband has his Master's Degree in Business and works for a shipping company. Economically, I would consider us to be in the high middle to upper class, yet with three children it is all spent. I am a white female my religion is Catholic.

Did "right"— I had three beautiful children. I am finally taking control of my life and going to school and realizing that it is very important to have goals for myself and attain them.

Do "over"— Not to have married at such an early age of 22 years old. Dated more people. I would have gone to college and also gotten my Master's degree.

Question asked — Do you feel that women in general take on more because if they didn't things would not get accomplished?

❖ ❖ ❖

Lou

I'm white, middle/upper-class white woman, 46 and single (no children), living in the midst of a large city. I am currently unemployed, but have held management positions in software companies for the last 18 years. I am a member of a non-denominational Christian church, would consider myself primarily a Democrat and have a BS in education.

Did "right"— I have made very good friends (many who have been with me for over 20 years) who have lived through many changes in my life. I have had the opportunity to travel extensively around the world, which taught me an appreciation for what I have in my life, the advantages of living in the US, and the beauty and wonder in the world.

Do "over"— I would have focused more on romantic relationships earlier in my life – would like to be married. Also, I would have taken the opportunity when I was younger to live in another country.

Question asked— To an older women – what do you believe is the most important factor in having a full, happy life?

What would you tell— To a younger woman – a very important focus in your life is your relationships with other people. Nurture them, believe in them, make time for them, grow with them.

—TEN YEARS LATER—

I'm now 55 years old (that is still a shocking number to me) and my life has changed pretty radically from my initial responses – in many ways! Initially, I was single and living and working in the city for over 20 years – now, I'm happily married, stepmother to 3 adult children (2 of whom live with us), living in a 'semi rural' community with a river in my backyard. I'm working at home for a large Fortune 500 company and managing many projects remotely. My workdays now consist of lots of emails and conference calls with people all over the world – but I can do that in shorts and t-shirts and go outside to pick a tomato from my garden for lunch. My husband and I are members of a Catholic church (which is the church that I attended all throughout my childhood). In fact, when I look at my initial responses, the only consistent items are that I'm still a Democrat and have a BS in Education – other than that, my world has changed rather radically! Marrying for the first time at the age of 48, moving away from the city and into a house with adult children has meant many adjustments, but every day, I feel that I am EXACTLY where I'm meant to be at this phase of my life. I've learned a lot about 'romantic' relationships (they take work, but are worth it – if you're with the right person and they are also willing to work at it) and parenthood (MUCH harder from the inside than the outside – I have a whole new appreciation for my parents and my siblings and friends with families who have made the parenthood process look SO EASY from the outside). I love my life now – and appreciate everything that's come before, since it was good preparation for where I am today.

***Did "right"**— My friends are still a HUGE part of my life, and having their support through all of the changes has been critical. And I still believe that travel has taught me appreciation for all that I have in my life. Since the last update, I had the opportunity to travel to Africa – and although I was lucky enough to go there on a very high end trip and was pampered all the way – it was clear that the advantages given to me based on the shear luck of being born and living in the US is a HUGE advantage in life.*

***Do "over"**— The old answers still apply – but looking back, I would add that I also would have started some therapy earlier in my life. Between some individual therapy that I started in my thirties, additional life training and sessions that I attended through education programs and other training, and the women leadership training/ support groups that I started attending when I was unemployed and* *have continued since then, I've learned a lot from other women's experiences and their perspectives on my experience.*

Question asked— *either younger, your age or older? I'd love to know what younger women think about the women who 'fought the fight' in the women's movement for the freedoms in the workplace and how that's affected their careers. For an older woman, I'd love to know what's helped them through the bumps in the road. Everyone has bumps – in their personal lives and in their careers, and it would be great to know what's been helpful to the women before me.*

What would you tell— *either younger, your age or older?*

It's been important to me to bond with other working women and get 'shots of courage' from them to help maneuver through the tricky work world. My friends have always been a big help, but the women's groups that I've joined in the last 10 years have added another level of support. The latest groups that I've worked with have included expert advice from executive coaches who've introduced new ideas and challenged everyone to push a little harder and be the best that they can – and that has been a huge help. It's assistance that I feel would be hugely helpful to a young woman starting in her career, and something that would have been helpful to me in my 30's.

❖ ❖ ❖

" I still believe that travel has
taught me appreciation for
all that I have in my life."

–Lisa

" I've sought counseling and reconciliation with family.
I'm dealing with my own problems; not allowing the
past to fester in the present thereby fouling the future."

–Adrien

in my 50's

" I'd tell them to live each day... don't wait until some mythical distant "sometime" future to live your dreams, but consider balance... don't forget about tomorrow either. Remember the old saying... those who fail to plan are planning to fail."
—Chris

Marty

50, married for 23 years with 3 children. The two oldest are boys, 17 and 15, the youngest is 13. I am looking forward to seeing my oldest go off to college next year, but will miss him. We live in a suburban turned urban area on a small peaceful lake. I am the most liberal in our household. My kids are shocked at some of my views. Now that my children are older I am gearing up to return to the workforce; I would like to do real estate appraisals. As an adult I have had to jump the hurdle of Bipolar in myself and one of my boys'. It has caused me (and others at times) a great deal of misery, but thank goodness for modern science!

Did "right"— I didn't get married until I was 26, and we waited to have children until 31. I have stayed at home, volunteered at the schools and in the community. My life is full. I pursue my convictions, take time to read, take a class here and there and spend time with my family. A little less traffic and "what's in it for me attitude" would be nice.

Do "over"— There are many things, big and small that I would do over if I could, get my degree, not be bipolar. The thing is, I have grown from all those painful experiences and they make a part of who I am today. Some small things would be – not to sweat the small stuff, listen better and create more hours in the day!

Question asked— Will there ever be a day when people stop killing people over religions?

What would you tell— Get a college degree. "Don't judge others until you have walked in their shoes." Everyone has the right to his or her opinions and way of life. People are entitled to personal decisions based on their beliefs. Respect that. Open your minds and hearts. Practice random acts of kindness. Appreciate, it could be gone tomorrow. Actively listen. Stay physically fit. You won't believe the aches and pains you'll have by 50 if you don't.

❖ ❖ ❖

Chris

50 and living in the suburbs of a west coast city, with my husband, of 32 months (first marriage) whom I met on the internet, and 2 cats (one is 20 years old and he's been with me since he was 8 weeks old and the other recently joined us about 3 months ago and is nearly 3 years old – and so far they don't like each other very much). I've recently reinvented myself as a travel agent/cruise consultant after bailing out of the graphic design biz and then being laid off from my job as a web producer/project manager for a dot-com a couple years ago. Having always loved travel, I'm enjoying this new career immensely, although so far "doing what I love" hasn't translated into much money — but at least I'm happy and having a great time... and my husband has been picking up the slack financially. We're pretty solidly middle class, although upwardly mobile as my business grows and as he builds seniority in his career as an IT specialist (now that the high tech biz seems to be making a comeback). We have no kids, but have discussed taking in foster children or perhaps adopting. With mixed Swedish/Irish heritage, I used to bill myself as the whitest woman in America, but I seem to tan more readily as I age. In general, I'm a committed liberal Democrat, in large part because I don't trust the motivations of the Republican leadership (and feel that many of the rank and file Republicans have been deceived and manipulated by them, but that's another story too long and sordid to go into here). I grew up in Washington, DC, during the turbulent 60's and 70's—civil rights, Vietnam, fighting to get 18 year olds the right to vote (something I'm not so sure I should have fought so hard for now), etc., and I've always had intense political leanings, although I suffered a long dormant period in the 70's following a crushing defeat. I have never failed to vote in a presidential election. I have a BA in media studies (communications), an AS in Hospitality/ Restaurant Management, and I recently went back to a local community college here to pick up some background in Travel.

Did "right"— I've had a lot of interesting experiences and overall I think they add up to the thing I've done "right" in my life – sampling and embracing everything. I've lived in a lot of places (Washington, DC, Virginia, Maryland, St. Louis, Salt Lake City, Las Vegas, Daytona Beach, Chicago, Mexico, Seattle and Portland). I also traveled as much as I could and have gotten to see a good part of the world, sampling many cultures and meeting people from all sorts of backgrounds. Now with the internet, I've expanded my "travels" and make personal contacts without even leaving home, and I have many friends all over the world that I keep in touch with. I find this fascinating and enriching (and it's how I met my Swedish husband). I've had several careers (secretary, waitress, bartender, restaurant manager, typesetter, graphic designer, copywriter, editor, project manager, medical marketing coordinator, webmaster, travel agent... heck, I even drove a Good Humor ice cream truck, worked in a styrofoam cup factory, was a phone sex operator briefly and posed nude for some art classes in my distant youth). Not all of these were positive experiences, but I learned a lot from all of them and I think that's a good thing.

Do "over"— If I could do anything over, I think I would have made plans and put a little more direction in my life. Maybe it was the times I grew up in, but I always liked the idea of just sort of drifting along and seeing what options popped up and then letting myself get swept along by events as they developed. Looking back, I would have lived my life more intentionally... planned better for my old age financially, directed my career a little more forcefully. Having never really wanted to get married or have children, I'm not sure I'd make the same decisions today now that I know how nourishing and positive true love actually is. I wish I'd figured that out earlier in life because on a lot of levels I feel cheated that I'll have 20 or 30 years with my husband instead of 40 or 50, and I have to admit that I do suddenly regret that children are not a realistic option at this point in my life (this from a girl who actually went to a doctor when I was 20 and asked to have my tubes tied (he turned me down, saying I would have to be married and have a note from my husband)!

Question asked— Do you know what you want to be when you grow up? And what are you doing to make that happen?

What would you tell— I would like to tell this to ANY young person (male or female). Learn everything you can about compound interest and put the principles of it to work for you NOW. Did you know (I heard this from an economist on a talk show) that if you put $2000 into an IRA account from the age of 18 until you're 28 and never contribute another dime, by the time you retire you will have a MILLION dollars? But if you wait until you're 28 and put $2000 in an IRA every year until you retire, you'll only have about $360,000? Even as a socialist hippie, if I'd known that when I was a kid, I'd have found a way to stash that $2K/yr and I'd be feeling a lot more secure as I move in on retirement age!

Also, I'd tell them to live each day… don't wait until some mythical distant "sometime" future to live your dreams, but consider balance… don't forget about tomorrow either. Remember the old saying… those who fail to plan are planning to fail.

❖ ❖ ❖

Sally

I am a white, 50 year old who lives in a suburban area outside a major east coast city. I have three children aged 26, 23, 21 and have been married 28 years. I am an active Unitarian, who has liberal leanings. I have a full time job as a billing manager, and we are in the upper middle to lower upper economic class. I have a BA degree and am currently working towards a certificate as a paralegal. I currently coach a girl's U12 soccer team. I have 15 years experience as a soccer coach (10 years boys, 5 years girls).

Did "right"— I encouraged my children to search and follow their own desires in life.

Do "over"— I would have applied and attended law school prior to having my children.

" The latest groups that I've worked with have included expert advice from executive coaches who've introduced new ideas and challenged everyone to push a little harder and be the best that they can – and that has been a huge help."

– Lisa

" Find a good friend who would tell you the truth."

– Lisa

Question asked— Is there a drastic change in energy from the 50's to 60's? What changes did you make in your lifestyle to adapt or limit this?

What would you tell— Things happen, some good, some bad. When you have a bad experience, try to learn from it, and then move on. There are always options! Many times we blind ourselves to choices right in front of us. Reach out; help usually comes from the most unexpected place. If you have a positive experience – ENJOY IT – keep it as a memory to use during a bad time.

❖ ❖ ❖

Bert

I'm in my early fifties, I live in a suburban town in the west coast, with my teenage son and my dog. I am divorced, work downtown, and manage to maintain an adequate albeit not lavish life style. I'm a college graduate, Caucasian, shun religion, and I'm a dedicated Democrat. I grew up in South America, but have lived in this country for more than 30 years.

Did "right"— Developed a strong sense of self.

Do "over"— I was in love when I got married, but, in a few short years, I fell out of love. I stayed in the marriage first out of a sense of duty, then because I had a child. I should have divorced when love turned to duty.

Question asked— What wisdom would you give me if I were to start another relationship?

What would you tell— Assess yourself along the way. Don't take your present life for granted. If you are where you want to be, look for a way to improve it; if you are not where you want to be, don't be afraid of change.

❖ ❖ ❖

Mattie

I am 52, urban, with a 17 year old teenager, widow, no work, no career, lower class, white, Presbyterian, democrat, some college.

Did "right"— 99.5% of the time I made people feel good about themselves.
—I let other people talk about themselves (whether I cared or not, they thought I did).
—I had the number of children I could handle.
—I was a great wife.
—I did well in the schools I attended.

Do "over"— Go to college for a specific career.
—Not gain weight.
—Get medical help sooner.
—Have more family doings/activities/outings. Cheap Fun.

Question asked— From an older woman—How does Medicare and Medicaid and Social Security work? What would she have done different after age of 65?

What would you tell— 95% of the time make your husband feel good about himself.
—Go to college for a specific trade.
—Don't leave the finances up to your husband.
—Have lots of family doings/activities/outings. Cheap Fun.

—TEN YEARS LATER—

Question asked— *What would she have done different after age of 65?*

Been able to see that many people my age were real drunks before I invested a lot of friend time into them. Realized that I had the choice of joining a group of people who only want to talk in a loud voice over everyone else all about themselves like at church or volunteer meetings. Or organized group parties or else sitting at home alone doing a craft or sitting on my couch. My 6 other friends are married and never have

*time to go to see a movie or art show or fair or something to do. They
have time to do these things with their other married couples.*

*Now I am a cripple can walk 35 steps at a time and have to sit down.
It may even effect my volunteering and then I will have nothing. I can
talk, drive for 15 minutes, have use of my senses and hands.*

❖ ❖ ❖

Lisa

I am 56 transplanted to a small town in the west coast. I was
married at the age of 20 and have two children with him and a 24
year marriage. My daughter is age 30 and son is age 28. Both are
married and living some distance away. I am now remarried for six
years to an old college sweetheart who I had not seen in 30 years.
My daughter is a recovering alcoholic-heroin addict. She is now
one-year clean. We are raising her 8-year old son. Not my plan for
retirement but such a blessing. My son is married and expecting
their first child, I have a college degree, I am conservative and
middle class.

Did "right"— Took the positive traits of my mother and
grandmothers and incorporated them into my life. I asked the Lord
into my life and allowed Him to lead me through the good and
the bad times.

Do "over"— There aren't many things I would do differently
(maybe rearrange some things a bit) because when I think about
my life, even the bad or rash decisions I've made had some kind
of link to a positive outcome. For instance marriage to a man who
turned out to be an abusive alcoholic, drug addict later in our
marriage gave me two beautiful children that I love and adore. I can't
imagine life without them.

The one thing that I most regret is an abortion I had when I was
very young. However, even that has had some good. It brought me

to a realization of how much I needed a Savior and no matter how good I tried to be, it wasn't enough. Nothing I do is beyond God's love and forgiveness. I've had a lot of boulders in my life. Today I might go around them in a little bit different way than in years past because of age and experience, however with each boulder or stone or pebble, I did the best I could with the resources I had available. Today I can look back on them and God has turned them into landscaping stones and I can see their beauty. He has used them – grown things around and on them.

Question asked— How do you deal with dramatic change in your life? How do you truly enjoy something and on the other hand how do you truly grieve something? How are the friends you have made late in life different from the friends you made when you were younger?

What would you tell— Find a good friend who would tell you the truth. Hope that you have both great joy in your life and great sorrow. Let God lead you through both. With Him your joy will make you beautiful and your sorrow will make you strong.

❖ ❖ ❖

in my 60's

" The relationships you have with others are in the long run, very important. These relationships you have are what make your life joyous or sad."
  –Gene

Alice

64 years old – I live on the west coast with my marvelous male partner.

I have three "kids". #1 a 42 year old daughter. She is married and they have a one-year-old son. She is a Special Ed. teacher in a middle school. I am middle-class, economically. #2 a 40 year old daughter who lives and works on the east coast. She is a vice-president of a huge company and is in the upper class financially. She is single and very career orientated. #3 is a 37 year old son who resides in the mid-west. He is married and has two daughters. He is the most successful in his profession and in the upper class financially.

I am a Caucasian, protestant (not attending any formal church), and politically lean a bit more to republican but vote for the most qualified person NOT party!! I attended 3 years of college and have owned three businesses, of which I was very actively involved.

Did "right"— Divorcing my first husband, learning about myself so I could become a good mother, like myself, set and accomplish goals, and finally choose a healthy, wonderful male partner.

Do "over"— I would choose other parents, as mine were dysfunctional and very abusive.

Question asked— The question I would ask another woman would be relating to her feelings about herself and her life.

What would you tell— I would like to tell another woman that until she feels good about herself life is a compromise and disappointing.

❖ ❖ ❖

Lorraine

I did not intend to become so philosophical about things, but I felt that this may be the only chance for someone to know what really concerns me and how I feel about life. I am a 64 year old. I live alone in a suburb of a large metropolitan area. Widowed a year after 24 years in a second marriage, I am beginning to re-discover the girl I once was. Although I miss my friend, my husband, I am enjoying this phase of my life. There is still incredible sadness but also the thrill of discovering new things about myself. I enjoy the quiet, not all the time, but most often. I have found comfort in making decisions for myself, not having to always consider someone else first. I worry about financial security; how long can I work full time; how long do I want to work full time; will I be able to perform to expectations... all are concerns that seem to manifest themselves more and more often.

There were no children of this marriage, however the first marriage of 20 years produced six children in eight years.

I was 18 when married the first time and had my first child at 19 and the last at 27. I am grateful to have had those children when I was young, physically active and what now is termed a stay-at-home mother. I have been very fortunate in my life to have the experience of being both a full-time mother until the youngest was in school as well as experiencing the totally different challenge and fulfillment of a successful professional career. The children (all Caucasian) range in age from 37 to 45, three boys and three girls.

Did "right"— I think I was/am a good mother who taught her children as I was taught. I love my children, even when I don't like them! I was very fortunate in being able to stay-at-home with my children until the youngest were in school full days. There were six born in eight years, the last before my 27th birthday. I was young enough to learn and grow up with them, they keep me young and in-tune with the world as they see it. I don't always agree with their views and worry about what the future will bring for all of us. I didn't always make the right decisions for them, but I always learned from those mistakes and tried to avoid errors in the future. They could always come to me with anything, even though they might have chosen not to. They lied and I didn't always acknowledge that I knew that, they needed to learn too. I was taught to do unto others, as you would have them do unto you. I have tried to live my life that way, not always being successful. I am proud to say that I taught my children common sense; you can have an education, but without common sense it may do you no good.

Do "over"— It's easy to look back, see your mistakes and think you would change parts of your life if you had the chance, but what happens to the knowledge you gained through those "mistakes?" Maybe if I could go back and change things, I wouldn't be the person I am today. Maybe, just maybe, those "do over" parts of my life enabled me to be able to help someone else, to make a difference. I may never know, but that does not matter. I would truly not change anything, even the darkest hours. I am comfortable with who I am; I'm not perfect and there is definitely room for improvement, but I like the person that I am. I want to be more serene, more peaceful and yet more vibrant, more full of life.

Question asked— Every question I wanted to ask someone older, I have asked my mother and been grateful to have that opportunity. I have talked to individuals my age about life's changes at this age so I can compare. I don't associate much with people my own age, not of choice, but circumstance. I remain working full time, have recently relocated to a new neighborhood and have few friends my own age. I always feel so much younger than those I do know. (I thank my children and grandchildren for that!) Sometimes I would like to ask younger families what the heck they are thinking! I worry a great deal about the lack of a true family life, not running from one sporting event to another or seeing each other at plays, school event, etc.. Do parents know what their children are thinking, not necessarily doing, although that is important as well? Sometimes I discuss the world with my young grandchildren and I know that their parents have not a clue what they are thinking. The depth of their understanding, when they do, is awesome and frightening!

The lack of understanding is just as shocking as some have no connection with "real world!" Television and other media have led them to harbor horribly incorrect versions and impressions of what life, love, and hate are all about. What will happen to these young people when they are finally in the world and on their own? Are they not set up for failure? Or worse, are they targets?

I would like to ask those who make policy decisions on what we see and what we don't see in the media, all media, what are they thinking? Where is the caring for one human being for another? Has the struggle for financial success overshadowed everything else?

Why can't we treat others how we would like to have them treat us?

—TEN YEARS LATER—

At 74 years of age; much has changed and yet remained the same. The death of my mother was a brutal blow. There is no one left now, who knew me as a young girl… I find that sad for me. I lost my best friend, my confidant and the most significant person in my life to the ravages of dementia. I sincerely pray that my children never will experience that particular circumstance of heartache. Death is a part of life, I know but it has made its presence known in the past months of my life with the loss of a younger sister and my firstborn grandson. I feel so adrift, as if I no longer belong to anyone. The loss has made me so very aware of my own mortality. I look forward to the rainbow that I know will once again break through the clouds of grief! Hurry!

I worked full time until early this year and retired; I no longer enjoyed the work process or the environment… there was no 'fun' anymore, no sense of accomplishment even though my pride in my work remained. The time to say 'Goodbye' to the work family had come. It has taken awhile to dismiss the feelings of guilt over falling asleep in the middle of the afternoon or watching a movie instead of doing the laundry! Or reading into the wee hours of the morning… or having a glass of wine for no reason except to enjoy it… how delightful! I can enjoy!

" I've had a lot of boulders in my life. Today I might go around them in a little bit different way than in years past because of age and experience, however with each boulder or stone or pebble, I did the best I could with the resources I had available."
  –Lisa

" I do however; strongly regret that addiction has reared its ugly head in the midst of my family. Nothing prepares you for the depth of that loss, the waste of life or the loss of the promise of a future."
  –Lorraine

My children today are between the ages of 55 and 47; there are 14 living grandchildren and 6 great-grandchildren! I congratulate myself on the opinions of my offspring expressed ten years ago as they hold true. Each has had his, or her, successes and challenges in life. I do however; strongly regret that addiction has reared its ugly head in the midst of my family. Nothing prepares you for the depth of that loss, the waste of life or the loss of the promise of a future.

I still worry about the seeming lack of true family life and I am so grateful that I sat at the table with my parents and siblings, every night for dinner. What great life lessons we discussed, the laughter, the sharing and caring! I don't think that happens so often in today's hectic lifestyles.

My grandchildren are my hope for the future; they are incredibly funny, inspiring, insightful, intelligent, ambitious, and ready for the rest of their lives! My impressions of them ten years ago remain… and that is both encouraging and frightening! They are by far, not perfect but not a one of us is. My advice to them and all their age; don't be afraid to venture out in the world and make mistakes, that's how you learn and you need to learn from each mistake and move forward. I still believe there is no replacing good old-fashioned common sense; I have met some truly brilliant individuals in my lifetime that hadn't a lick of common sense and will never overcome. I still venture out for new things to learn!

I remain steadfast in that even in the darkest hours of my 74 years, I would not change anything in my life. The good, the bad, and the ugly have contributed to the person I am today. I'm not crazy about the image in the mirror, but I am comfortable and proud of the person I have become. I will do all I can to remain as healthy as I can be; strive to be a more serene and peaceful individual; remain vibrant and full of life and retain my sense of humor as I move through the latter years of my age. I think those latter years will demand a sense of humor! Bring them on!

❖ ❖ ❖

Darcy

I am divorced, 65 year old woman. A devout Christian. I lost a son
to suicide, which is still very difficult to accept. I teach pre-school,
am a poet, and honest, caring and strong. I presently found a soul
mate and enjoy the company of a male.

What would you tell— It's not what happens to you, but what you
do with what happens to you. It's not what actually happens, but
what you perceive as happening. It's not the event, but the meaning
attached to the event.

I would add that our ability to attach meanings to events requires
being quiet, building spaces for reflection, and listening with open
hearts to what God has to say to us. Only then can we ask the right
questions of ourselves, questions, which help us, understand the
paths we need to follow.

—TEN YEARS LATER—

*In light of my comments ten years ago my belief is stronger than ever.
It truly is not what you experience in life but your perception of it, held
close, which determines your path.*

*When I was twelve and then again at thirteen an illness put me at death's
door. In the hospital bed, I felt a glowing light above me as I was lifted into
comforting arms and heard the words, "it's ok, it's not time for you to come
with me yet." Oh, how I wanted to stay with him, but he put me back into
my body. And so today I still see what God wants me to do and I think this
experience prompted my words ten years ago.*

*Although the soulmate mentioned earlier is no longer with me, my
concentration on quiet time, Bible Study, and listening to God with
an open heart remains. Not being true to my values and personal
boundaries is how that relationship failed. Questions I have been
asking myself lately include these: "Am I being all God wants me to
be?" and, "What do I need to change?"*

One change I have made is living with my sister in another state. Since she is five years younger than I, we've never had a chance to know each other well. Her caring and support plus that from long-standing friends in the area, connecting with my daughter and her family more often makes the best possible situation. I've also found a supportive church, one full of joy. More time for me involves writing (a book of poetry and a memoir which I will be sending to publishers). Oh yes, it's work too, but so fulfilling. Art projects satisfy my creative urge: snipping bits of color from magazines pages making designs. Life is good.

❖ ❖ ❖

Charlotte

I'm 68 years old, I have three children, and five grand children. I live in the suburbs of a large mid-western city. I'm Presbyterian, middle-upper class. I live with my husband, and we have been married for 46 years. My work is financial management for my home and bookkeeping for my husband's business.

Did "right"— I had three wonderful children, and married a very happy person. I've tried to put God as number one in my life and the gift of faith, surrendered my will to God and persevered. I feel I have been a good support system.

Do "over"— Make a point to make a niche for myself, something to call my own. To have concentrated on a small area of my life— throughout my entire life.

Would have gone to a small all girls college, to be more of a student in college, not to be so side tracked by men.

Question asked— *For older women*—What do you value the most in your life?

What would you tell— To concentrate on the areas you have some control over and let go of the areas you cannot control.

" It's easy to look back, see your mistakes
and think you would change parts of
your life if you had the chance, but what
happens to the knowledge you gained
through those mistakes?"
–*Lorraine*

" I would like to tell another woman that
until she feels good about herself life is
a compromise and disappointing."
–*Alice*

—TEN YEARS LATER—

Changes in the last 10 years – my health – I've had several strokes at about age of 70. I had boundless energy up to that time, also I had many wonderful friends that have either died or moved away. Fortunately, my family: children, grandchildren, and husband are all intact. I am blessed by living in and loving our home of 40-plus years. However, even our home has changed. I love to decorate, so every year I make changes to it. My faith is still very strong, even though we have gone from an upper middle class family to I do not know what... not richer for sure. Tips to live by: No other Gods before me and live in today with a passion.

❖ ❖ ❖

Paige

I am 69, white middle class, I have a masters degree and additional graduate courses, English teacher, I am a Christian, have four daughters and divorced.

Did "right"— Raised four wonderful daughters and three are wonderful mothers and one a very special aunt.

Do "over"— I would have never married for the second time. I would have paid more attention to how my children felt when they were growing up. I didn't even think about how they felt when I made decisions.

Question asked— I would ask how you resolve competitive issues with other women?

What would you tell— I would tell another woman to pay attention to their children's feelings... It is especially important to focus on what the children are feeling as those instances shape human beings. I would tell them to let go of their children when they become adults. There is nothing more harmful than controlling mothers.

—TEN YEARS LATER—

*It is interesting when I look back on what I wrote over nine years ago.
I am 78 now. I am teaching courses at a community college (still).
And very busy. My family has added one more person to it, one of
my granddaughters is married now. A beautiful wedding. I have five
grandchildren out of college, one still in college and one entering high
school… so life brings good changes. My youngest sister died two years
ago and that was quite a shock. She went to the hospital, had surgery,
and died during surgery. It makes one think of all the unspoken words
to one who is loved. She was only 69 years old… far too young to leave
her three daughters. My other younger sister is moving from the family
home, so another big change. Three of my daughters are all doing well
in their jobs. Another daughter is busy and involved with her three
children…. My daughters are strong women. I am proud to call them
my children.*

Do "over"— *Same as nine and a half years ago EXCEPT I have paid
more attention to my children since then and I have totally accepted
them as they are. EACH is strong and independent…*

Question asked— *I guess it would be to ask women why they spend so
much time thinking of their age and getting older. It is inevitable. Why
be afraid of getting older? Of dying?*

What would you tell— *Pay attention to their young and adult
children's feelings. Laugh at the mistakes. Don't be defensive. Let
them be who they are. Expect NOTHING but their love and you will
reap rewards. Children are a gift from God and a true blessing and
every worry and angst is worth every minute of one's life. Don't beat
yourself up for the mistakes we ALL make. Life is short and live it and
accept it.*

❖ ❖ ❖

in my 70's

" If you can be honest with yourself as well as all others you will,
ultimately, have a good life."

–Gene

Betty

I am 74 years old and a widow living in a townhouse in a suburb
of a large city. I have three grown sons ages 48, 46 and 43. Two are
married and one divorced. One of them owns his own business, one
works for a large corporation and the other works in estate planning
and retail. We are all middle class. All Caucasian, all Protestant and
most of us are Republicans. I have two years of college. One son has
two years of college and the other two graduated from college. I have
seven wonderful grandchildren. Each one holds a special place in
my heart, as they are all different. I was born in Canada. Have lived
on both the west coast and east coast. Also lived three years in Hong
Kong.

Did "right"— Became a Christian!

Do "over"— That is a double edge question.

(a) Because it was so exciting? Ride camels & elephants. Visit the
Taj Mahal and sit and marvel at its beauty. See the sun set on The
Gateway To India. Walk on the Great Wall again. Just experience the
wonderful smells & sights & excitement of Asia.
(b) Because I could do better? Raise my children with the wisdom I
have now!

Question asked— Another woman older or same age – What in
your life has made you content or unhappy?

What would you tell— To live a life of integrity knowing in your
heart you have done your very best.

—TEN YEARS LATER—

*I am now an almost 84 year old widow and this has been the decade
of change. Hard to believe but I have been told that when you reach
80 things do begin to happen. It is as if someone hit the fast forward
button and you better hang on and enjoy the ride.*

The "same's" are I still have 3 sons now 10 years older. New: One still owns his own business, one is now retired and one has left western side of the state and now lives in eastern side of the state. Grandchildren are growing quickly. Two have graduated from college. Three should graduate this coming year and my youngest will be entering high school. I see their lives really changing and I love watching their adventures.

Now for my life: I sold my townhouse, which had housed all my family at one time or another. I downsized and moved into a new condo right in the downtown area thinking that would be my forever move. Lived there for 6 years and truly found it exciting to be where the action was. In my early 80's realized that perhaps retirement home living would be a good idea so I began looking and researching. My sons were not happy about the decision however after coming with me to see a few places realized that life could be fun and stimulating and help was available when needed. That was the biggest decision I made during these past 10 years. It was done with a lot of prayer, thought and research. That was 9 months ago and I can honestly say I know it was the right move for me. I will be the first to admit Retirement Living is not for everyone. For me it is a good fit. I do not have long term care insurance so to be in a place that will take care of me forever is a big relief for me and my family. Moving here has been a huge gift for my sons. They can enjoy their lives without having to worry about me. I still drive my car and pretty much live as I did when I had my condo. I attend my church on Sundays I attend my Bible Study and have my social life as before. But I have this wonderful security net when needed. I have been blessed with good health except for the normal aging process. This has been the decade of change and my advice is Let Us Rejoice and Be Glad In It.

The rest of the questions are pretty much the same. Becoming a Christian certainly was a "right" and good thing to do. Oh, what would I do without my faith.

❖ ❖ ❖

Gene

I am a widow in my mid 70's. My husband and I raised three sons. I presently live in Florida and Maine and "dating" a man who also is widowed and much like my beloved husband. I finished school in my late 40's graduating from college. I have been a store detective, Republican Committee Woman and a delegate to the Republican Conventions several times. I love to sing, am in the church choir and am a devout Methodist.

Did "right"— The three most important events in my life:
1) My marriage.
2) The birth of my children.
3) The death of my husband.

Do "over"— I have no regrets in my life.

What would you tell— The three things I would tell other women:

The relationships you have with others are in the long run, very important. These relationships you have are what make your life joyous or sad.

If you can be honest with yourself as well as all others you will, ultimately, have a good life.

To have faith in God and living your life in that truth will complete you as a person.

❖ ❖ ❖

" I would add that our ability to attach meanings to events requires being quiet, building spaces for reflection, and listening with open hearts to what God has to say to us. Only then can we ask the right questions of ourselves, questions, which help us, understand the paths we need to follow."

–Darcy

part two | questions:

you asked

you answered

Wants to know what is your best personality trait?

Sherri (20's) My depth of caring for those I love.

Diana (20's) My ability to love and care for others in need.

Karrie (20's) I am a good listener. I am willing and able to be open and honest in conversations. There is not a lot that I hold back. I guess you could say my best trait is communication.

Adrian (30's) My organizational skills. Helps me out in many different parts of my life.

Penny (40's) Encourager, cheerleader, enthusiastic.

Kylie (40's) I am constant, stick things out and very loyal to friends and family.

Mary (40's) Optimism.

Mattie (50's) The ability to make people genuinely happy to talk to me. It is a honed craft. Years of experience. In other words I can get people talking, normally about themselves and they feel good to tell me whatever they are talking about.

Lorraine (60's) The ability to laugh at myself and with others, and in some cases to make others laugh. I was blessed with a family who laughed a lot. That sense of humor has never failed me!

Betty (70's) Outgoing, friendly, loves people.

❖ ❖ ❖

I would like to ask an older women what should I do now to be successful later in life?

Kylie (40's) Evaluate yourself, get to know yourself so that you can make choices that are congruent with who you are. You may have to ask friends to help you with this process so that there is complete honesty. I really feel strongly about education... whatever that may look like in your field – whether trade school, university... whatever it takes to have the skill sets to succeed in your field. Be flexible...

Mary (40's) Get an education so that you can do something that you enjoy – not something that you have to do to earn a living.

Mattie (50's) Learn people skills and learn conversation skills. Learn how not to talk too much (monopolizing), learn how to 'throw the ball of conversation' back and forth. Learn how to stop an argument before it comes to a head. Learn how to make people feel good about themselves.

Lorraine (60's) Learn from your mistakes, everything is a learning experience of some kind, don't forget the lessons. Mistakes without lessons for the future mean you keep repeating the same ones, how boring. If you are lucky, you will meet and have a friend who will be a mentor, learn from your mentor.

Betty (70's) Take time daily for some quiet time with the Lord. Oh I know when your life is full and busy that doesn't seem possible or important but believe me it is. You will be able to accomplish so much more. You will be led in the right direction. You will be able to succeed.

❖ ❖ ❖

I always love to hear the stories of older women and how they encountered difficulties in their lives and how they overcame them.

Sherri (20's) By remembering that all events/feelings are temporary and will pass at some time. My difficulties are very ordinary: figuring out what and who I love determining whether my feelings are/can be reciprocal.

Kylie (40's) Prayer and healthy friendships... also a lot of reading. A good friend once said a problem is something that is always outside of yourself (because if you knew the answer it wouldn't be a problem) so continually seek the right (which means listening to your inner-voice...) sources for information.

Mary (40's) Wow – do you have a day or two – generally speaking I would say being optimistic and having faith that things will work out if you don't get discouraged.

Mattie (50's) I encountered death of a spouse. No quick fix for overcoming. Days taking you away from The Day is the only thing that makes it better. Keeping your mouth shut is another good trick. You can pour out to a good friend but not to EVERYONE who will listen. Expect to be not over it for 4-5 years. Don't make any big moves with things or money. No matter how much you think you are in control... you aren't.

Paige (60's) Therapy. Friends help. Important to develop life long friends. You can learn a lot from a friend of 20, 30, 40 plus years. You only have one to three friends that become family. You learn to trust them, they trust you. If you go to therapy and church you can take what you learn and bounce it off a trusted friend. Families have dynamics that often prohibit one from seeing the situation objectively. That is why it is vital to have trusted friends and not change friends so often. Having a lot of friends often prevents you from seeing yourself honestly.

Betty (70's) Yes, stories are a testimony and an encouragement. My difficult time was when my husband was returning from a business trip and died suddenly of a heart attack on an airplane. I could not believe the telephone call informing me of what had happened. I was at home alone in a foreign country. Fortunately I had a wonderful church family to call upon. Those beautiful Christian women surrounded me with love. The whole thing was a nightmare and it was only my strong Christian belief that brought me through all the trials and turmoil that followed.

❖ ❖ ❖

What are you most proud of in your life and what would you still like to change in your life that you haven't been able to tackle?

Sherri (20's) I am always proud that I'm an aware, observant person. This sensitivity also means that it's very easy for my emotions to detrimentally overwhelm me.

Karrie (20's) I am most proud of the accomplishments, which include my daughter, my schooling and overall how far I've made it at this point in my life being a single mother.

Adrian (30's) Proud? My good relationship with my husband. We've been married 14 years and each year our marriage grows deeper. Change in my life? I wish for heavens sake that I could stop overeating and indulging in too many sweets. Maintaining weight is a major struggle.

Penny (40's) That I'm independent, can get most anything done that I put my mind to, EXCEPT carrying on a life-time intimate relationship. That is frustrating for me since it is something I desire and I think helps me grow.

Kylie (40's) My kids, my home, my family, my church, my education, my students. As far as doing over I need to prioritize my husband more! I need to learn how to love him for who he is not what I want him to be. Acceptance.

Mary (40's) Most proud of my children – want to go back to school and have not succeeded with that yet – I said yet.

Lorraine (60's) I am most proud of my accomplishments as a mother. Each of my children is different, not all are what society would term "successful," but each is a distinct human being with something to offer the world. Together they are alike and yet different, each in his, or her, own way. They are amazing. I want to be more serene, I have a dear friend who 'marches to the tune of a different drummer' who is the most serene individual I have ever met. I want that serenity, and have no idea yet how to accomplish that. That's the challenge of life; I can still learn and can't wait!

Betty (70's) Proud of my three loving sons. Not only their love and thoughtfulness toward me but their love for each other. Their respect and acts of kindness towards those they meet and know. Want to change? Hard to say at this stage of my life. I know what I don't want to change and that is my sense of humor! I can even make myself laugh sometimes.

❖ ❖ ❖

I would not ask for her advice, because who knows if I would listen. I would not ask for her opinion, but I would ask her to tell me about her life and then I would listen.

Lorraine (60's) You know what, you would find that her life is not so different from your own. Listen to your own inner voice, I bet you find the pathway to a person you admire.

Betty (70's) Many times it's just best to tell "your" story. Others can decide to use the information or forget it. We don't need to tell others what to do with their lives unless we are asked.

❖ ❖ ❖

How do you maintain a separate identity in a marriage (especially with children)?

Adrian (30's) I don't worry so much about maintaining a separate identity. I am me, and I certainly have my own identity, but who I am is also so tied to my role as wife and mother.

Kylie (40's) I have been blessed with a husband who has allowed that. Perhaps I have been very persistent, he gave me advice that at first I thought was awful, but now I want to share it... "you have to take it, it won't be given to you" apply that as you will, but it helped me get through graduate school!

" Evaluate yourself, get to know yourself so that you can
make choices that are congruent with who you are."
– *Kylie*

" I have owned up to my mistakes and tried to make
them right. I suit up and show up for the people
who need me. I ask for help. I ask for help a lot."
– *Carlie*

Mary (40's) That is tough to do – not so much with my husband because he is very "behind the scenes" but with my kids I don't really have a life other than sharing theirs right now. But that's okay with me right now.

Mattie (50's) Keep God number one in your life, then your spouse, then you then your children. Don't engulf yourself so much in your kids. You will always have time for you and YOUR doings.

Charlotte (60's) By having an authentic self, by truly being me. I get that by spending a lot of time looking within.

❖ ❖ ❖

Where do you want to go back too?

Sherri (20's) Junior high – I would've averted events/feelings that have made me cynical and jaded about human nature.

Adrian (30's) I wish my hometown was closer than it is over 800 miles away. I don't get back there too often.

Penny (40's) Many places, but I think that my attraction to them had to do not so much with the PLACE, but with the people there and the circumstances.

Kylie (40's) Having little babies... I want to cuddle them, and spoil them and not worry about life but just absorb them!

Mary (40's) Today – I want to go back to bed.

Betty (70's) *Country* – Ireland and Asia; *Time* – When my children were babies. Now that is a precious time.

❖ ❖ ❖

What don't you know yet?

Sherri (20's) Everything.

Adrian (30's) I don't know how to help someone who seems to be making poor life choices. I wish I knew how to get them to want to change their own life decisions. (I'm thinking here about my younger sister who has chosen a life of drug abuse and has been in and out of jail. Why? I've never tried drugs, and I've never done anything to be in trouble with the law).

Kylie (40's) How to get out of debt! How to increase my income without changing my lifestyle... any thoughts?

Mary (40's) Some days I think I know it all and some days I don't think I know anything – there will always be something I don't know so don't sweat it.

Betty (70's) Are you kidding? It's what DO I really know.

❖ ❖ ❖

Wants to know how older women can maintain a young playful heart as responsibilities grow in your life?

Kylie (40's) Hang out with younger people... my husband is older than I am and it has worked for him... but it is killing me so I have adopted his policy. I look for other youthful people to play with! Don't stop playing! Stay active, it will make a huge difference later on in live!

Mary (40's) Always be in touch with young people especially children - they can teach us a lot about being young at heart

Roberta (50's) If you can chose to ignore certain casual remarks of age—do so.

Play is not the opposite of work. It is the attitude with which we enjoy the company of others.

So, when around "others," refrain from encouraging remarks about how you are so young with regard to this 'n that; or, saying that another is young or old about this 'n that. Participating in this adage supports separatism and isolation, creating good/bad dichotomies. In other words, don't allow anyone to put an age requirement on being corny, silly, naive or dramatic. If an older person remarks how you are so young... blah, blah, blah...don't accept it! Enjoy them, not their naive indulgences on what another said to them.

By accepting these remarks you infer agreement to the gossipy divisions of young vs old; good vs bad – and it WILL come back to haunt you later, making you feel isolation is the norm, thereby interfering with your instincts to be "light and silly, enjoying a funny cloud in front of a rain storm."

Don't participate in the "age comments" about memory or appearances. Accept what you can remember and enjoy asking others what they can recall – no matter what the age of the person you are speaking to. Do not apologize for who you are, only for who you knew you should be. Laugh at yourself. Be ageless in your love for the companionship of others.

❖ ❖ ❖

Where do you go when you have nothing to say?

Sherri (20's) In a conversation when you're speechless, I always ask questions of the other person until something they say piques my interest.

Adrian (30's) Prayer.

Kylie (40's) I listen and then pray.

Mary (40's) I never have "nothing" to say.

❖ ❖ ❖

Would you tell another person's secret and if so who would you tell and why?

Sherri (20's) Only if the secret needed to be told for health/ security reasons.

Adrian (30's) Yes, if that person was involved in abusive situations.

Kylie (40's) NEVER! I have told my teenagers if they tell me stories I do not want names because I will have to tell their parents. Unless it is life threatening. It has worked, we don't gossip but have a lot of funny stories!

Mary (40's) That really depends on the situation.

Betty (70's) Never Except if someone was considering suicide and then I would call family and/or a Dr. to get the help needed immediately.

❖ ❖ ❖

How did you decide whether or not to have children?

Adrian (30's) My husband and I waited until we both said, I'm ready. That took over 6 years of marriage. And if we ever got to the point that we were not both ready at the same time, we would have remained childless. As it is, we've taken the unusual role of choosing to only have one child.

Kylie (40's) I didn't, it just happened, personally that would be a hard decision to have to make.

Mary (40's) I just knew.

Mattie (50's) JP Morgan was once asked how much a yacht cost to have, and he replied that if you had to ask then you couldn't afford one in the first place. Well if you have to ask if you should have kids or not I would say don't have them.

❖ ❖ ❖

How do you cope with the unknown? And what advice would you give to not let the unknown cloud today's happiness?

Sherri (20's) You cope by accepting you're powerlessness. Then you do a good job controlling what you can.

Penny (40's) I'm trying to put emphasis on the verb, to be more trusting of the Lord instead of trying to understand why things happen. I think when we're pleased with something we are grateful to God, but when things don't make sense we get angry instead of trusting that things are going the way they are intended.

Kylie (40's) I have learned that just about all of life is unknown, and just when you think you know it... it changes again. I am not a flexible person but have to pray for it daily. I am learning that the joy is really in the unknown and that we constantly need to surrender to God and let Him be in control. A lot of prayer time and quiet daily devotions keeps me knowing that it is not unknown to HIM!

Mary (40's) Again, optimism.

Mattie (50's) Age old adage "Don't borrow trouble". There are no crystal balls. Stick with your walk with Jesus and he will get you through the troubles you might encounter.

Charlotte (60's) I have faith... and say it will work out... trust! You Grow Up!

Betty (70's) I put my life in Gods hands.

❖ ❖ ❖

Wants to know if it is true that when your kids are ready to leave home, you are ready for them to leave home?

Sherri (20's) Speaking from experience, the more you let go, the more your kids will come back to you. If you cling, your relationship will remain as parent:child rather than evolving naturally to parent:adult.

Kylie (40's) I have a daughter leaving for college in a week, and I have to say–Yes. She is so ready, not because she isn't scared, but because it is the right and healthy thing to do. It is funny all the

" Grab every opportunity, but as you do pay attention
to those you might be leaving behind."
  –*Nicole*

" Get stressed out, it's ok, especially about the little things. Those
are the things when you look back, that were big. Learn to love
everything. If you think the rain is a horrible inconvenience,
go play in it." – *Carlie*

transitions they go through... preschool, kindergarten, 6th grade and high school all prepare you for this moment. Each of those is hard and special in their own way. It doesn't mean I won't miss her, everyday I miss having my little girl to play with, but I know it is the right time. Plus, I have new adventures to look forward to, we like to travel together and so I know the Lord will put that in our future!

Mary (40's) I asked that question and some days I know that I will be and some days it breaks my heart to think about a day without them.

Lorraine (60's) Yes and no. I had six, although I was ready for each to begin their own life's journey, I was sad to see them leave the nest. I cried every time one of them left, for totally different reasons each time. I can't describe why, you will find out for yourself. My experience may not be yours.

Betty (70's) You are usually ready and so are they. It is called letting go. First they go off to college where they are gone but not out of the house forever because they have their haven to return to. You and they have 4 years to get used to that kind of leaving home. That makes the final move out easier. But be ready for them to return! It does happen.

❖ ❖ ❖

How do you teach your children to handle stress?

Sherri (20's) By example!

Adrian (30's) We've been teaching our son, to take a personal break. Take a deep breath, close your eyes, and let muscles relax. It has seemed to help him. He's only 7 and will tell us he needs to take a break.

Kylie (40's) By example, if I could do over I would have seriously looked at how I communicated my stress. I was pretty stressed out during graduate school and communicated it not in the most positive way. Looking back I wish I had seen the long-term effects of that.

Mary (40's) I don't know that yet.

Mattie (50's) Stress with kids – don't load them up in the first place. So when stress comes they have room to handle it. Teach them breathing techniques ahead of time.

Lorraine (60's) Not always by example, believe me. I still (in my sixties) fail miserable to 'handle' stress on occasion, but that's what life is all about isn't it? Success and failure and trying to improve on it.

Betty (70's) Children watch you so it's important to be a good example. Always try to talk to them about their life then when they are under stress and have problems they will share that with you. That is your opportunity to share your experiences and try to help them.

❖ ❖ ❖

How do you deal with relatives (husbands, mothers, mother-in-laws) who try to control your life?

Sherri (20's) Women are too nice and too worried about appearing mean. Sometimes it is very appropriate to be mean.

Adrian (30's) With gentleness and grace. Ask God to help you draw clear lines. In a good tone of voice and as gentle as possible, say thank you for your advice and then proceed however you and husband decide together.

Mary (40's) I stand my ground, pick my battles.

Kylie (40's) Unfortunately I moved away (2,000 miles), because I could not deal with it. The long run is I do not have family near me. Looking back I wish I was more assertive and willing to take the painful moments of truth so that in the long run we would be physically closer. However, I still have a close relationship with my Mom and Dad, via cell phone. I talk with them daily. This relationship now works (just large phone bills).

Lorraine (60's) When you are younger it seems so important to let people know that they can't or won't control your life. As you grow older you realize that you allow or don't allow that to happen. It is only important that you can look into the eyes of the person in the mirror and like her, are proud of her, and know that she did the best she could most of the time. Who can control that? Only you.

Betty (70's) Sweetly and firmly.

❖ ❖ ❖

How do you adjust to your husband's family when you've been raised so differently?

Sherri (20's) Learn about their culture and understand their perspective.

Diana (20's) Take it all in stride and try to learn from the good portions that you wish your parents would have included and try to learn from the mistakes that you think were made in his raising so you will not make them raising your own family. Don't try to change anyone, it will just hurt you in the end, just learn and teach.

Kylie (40's) I think this is a big way in which God helps all of us to grow up. There are many things his family does that drive me nuts, but I have to admit there are many things my family has lacked so I have tried to adopt the good and learned to let go of the bad. Anger is a huge issue with my husband and it has spilled into my children so that is one area that we will probably have to work on for years until we break the generational habit.

I guess look how the good can counter balance the bad. Also, look how his bad can sometime secretly be your good... and take hold

" Don't hold grudges, get past how you feel about
things and find out the facts – it saves a lot of
time to get to the truth quickly and past what
you perceive to be true."

–Liz

" I'd tell them to live each day... don't wait
until some mythical distant 'sometime'
future to live your dreams."

–Chris

of it and enjoy not adopting your family of origins patterns, but your new family's values… the exciting thing is you can always tell your parents that you are doing it for harmony when in fact you like it better!

Mary (40's) Just try to remember that they were a different type of family, doesn't mean it was wrong just different.

Lorraine (60's) Realize that they have the right to their own background. It doesn't have to change you or your marriage. It can enrich it if you let it. They have great stories to tell even if they are so diverse and different from your own. They influenced the man you married, there's a thought for you!

Betty (70's) It's not always easy. Even when both families have the same value system we all approach things differently. Try to remember in a lot of things there isn't a right way or a wrong way, just a different way.

❖ ❖ ❖

Do you feel that women in general take on more because if they didn't things would not get accomplished?

Sherri (20's) No, if women did less, others would pick up the slack. This is a common, detrimental "martyr" syndrome.

Lynn (30's) Yes, because I think part of the problem has to do with the feminist movement – we've gotten a better place in the work force, but we have never redefined the roles at home. In essence we are now taking on too much. The truth is we like the roles of homemaking, nurturer, but we are stretching ourselves too thin. We need to redefine the roles at home.

Mary (40's) Yes and sometimes I think we just feel like if we want it done right do it ourselves, but sometimes I think that saying should be changed to "if you want it done the way you want it done then just do it yourself" – sometimes you have to let others come to the same end point, but maybe they don't get there the same way that you do doesn't mean it's wrong just different.

Kylie (40's) Yes, but it has nothing to do with getting things accomplished, but more out of fear. We are afraid to confront our families that we need help, afraid to make our children unhappy, afraid to make our bosses unhappy, and the list goes on. So what we do instead is make ourselves miserable. We need to be more willing to fight the battle up front, say that we are worth it and we need help. Unfortunately, that is much easier said than done.

Charlotte (60's) Not as much in my generation... they cook and grocery shop. It is different than when you were younger, perhaps it has to do with energy.

Betty (70's) Yes!

❖ ❖ ❖

How have you dealt with disappointment?

Sherri (20's) By setting new goals.

Penny (40's) Try to do things that are fun and make me happy. Looking forward, not back. Being grateful for what I DO have instead of dwelling on what I don't have.

Kylie (40's) Trusting that it is God's plan for me to grow from. I have also had to make sure that the discussion of what I am disappointed about is out on the table and truth is around it so that I can move forward.

I think also accepting that disappointment is part of life. I think we spend way too much time not letting our kids get disappointed as opposed to teaching them how to deal with disappointments.

Mary (40's) I cried, quit, ignored it – but most of all I try to think there is a reason for it (those rose colored glasses again).

Betty (70's) Accepted it but didn't let it get me down.

❖ ❖ ❖

What have been your greatest joys apart from having children?

Sherri (20's) Good, close friendships.

Adrian (30's) Spending time with my husband. Going to college and getting my degree. Knowing and loving Christ Jesus as my Lord and Savior.

Kylie (40's) So many, my home, my education, painting, reading, swimming, nature, cooking, serving, traveling, fellowship... so many!!!

Betty (70's) Having grandchildren. Now that's a "joy." Also having the opportunity to serve the Lord even in small ways.

❖ ❖ ❖

Do you know what you want to be when you grow up? And what are you doing to make that happen?

Sherri (20's) I know the general direction; I'm educating myself.

Kylie (40's) Help, I keep thinking I do but then it changes. Recently, I have been praying to be transparent so that God can work through me. Maybe that?

Betty (70's) A patient person and what am I doing about it – trying.

❖ ❖ ❖

If you lived your identity through your roles (ie mother, wife...) who would you be now?

Sherri (20's) In this culture you would probably be what you do: a doctor, designer, counselor.

Adrian (30's) I would probably be a missionary in a foreign country. Or perhaps a foreign language translator.

Kylie (40's) Still way too many. Mom, business women, educator, cook, friend, painter.

❖ ❖ ❖

If you were 42 again what would you do differently?

Sherri (20's) Exercise and eat better (I'm guessing...).

Kylie (40's) I am 42 and I guess I wish I wasn't so insecure and doubting my past and future.

Betty (70's) Stop trying to be a perfectionist. We don't have to be Mrs. Clean.

❖ ❖ ❖

What do you believe is the most important factor in having a full, happy life?

Sherri (20's) Good relationships.

Adrian (30's) Have a personal relationship with Jesus. John 3:16

Penny (40's) People! Invest in and enjoy the relationships in life.

Kylie (40's) Faith in God that everything is according to His purpose and His plan for your life is good and tailor made for you.

Betty (70's) For me personally it is my belief and faith in Jesus Christ. That is my firm foundation, my rock. That is where my deep down joy comes from. Happiness happens but that joy securely locked in my heart enables me to thrive and survive in any and all circumstances.

❖ ❖ ❖

How do you deal with dramatic change in your life?

Sherri (20's) You don't linger or dwell on the past.

Adrian (30's) Pray, cry, call a good friend.

Kylie (40's) I would echo Adrian... pray, cry (don't under estimate the power of tears... it's okay) and call a good friend.

Mary (40's) you just have to I hate it but you can't change it if it's something you can't control – if I can control it so as not to be so drastic all at once I'll cross fire to do that – for instance this is trivial but I really wanted to go with short hair but my hair has been so long for so long that it took me a year to gradually do it, and I love it but had I done it all at once I would have absolutely hated it.

Lorraine (60's) Sometimes it isn't easy. Sometimes you don't want to. Sometimes you fight it. Then reality sets in and you realize that all things must happen for a reason, some big plan by some Supreme Being, we many never know why for a long time, if ever. Acceptance is a difficult thing to learn, very difficult when you are young, the older you get, the more you realize that if it is meant to be it will be. Without being preachy,' faith is a great friend to rely on. I found grief to be by far the most dramatic and difficult change in my life.

Betty (70's) Change doesn't come easy for me so I really have to work through it a bit at a time.

❖ ❖ ❖

How do you truly enjoy something and on the other hand how do you truly grieve something?

Sherri (20's) You enjoy something when you are fully in the moment, in the present. You are open-minded to the situation. You grieve by putting memories in their proper place, not reliving them but accepting them.

Kylie (40's) I think the only way you can do that is to be in the moment. When we live our life simply in the today, we will find all those emotions. But by living in the moment of joy we can fully experience it, and by grieving when it calls for that (not when we impose it) we can feel it and let it go. It is a huge struggle and will take a life altering experience to make you understand this, but that is the only way I can deal with pure joy and pure pain. Live in the moment! Do not project either joy or pain, that projection will disappoint and shatter you!

Lorraine (60's) I am truly happy to be alive; life is a challenge, relish in it. If you do, you will know how you truly enjoy something. On the other hand, grief is a difficult, complex emotion and one I have yet to understand or master. In the beginning it is resident, you are never without it, it feels terminal. It's a black hole. Then one day the 'fog' lifts a little and you realize that life had provided a measure of insulation that you hadn't realized. Life begins again, not that it really stopped, but it felt like it. Little things make you laugh again and really mean it. Children and grandchildren are great medicine. Friends who understand, give you a hug when you need it, and make you laugh are precious. Then when you think you are 'better' it sneaks up on you again when you least expect it. One lonely tear will force the break in the dam and they all fall! But the memories are the way to heal. Good memories and the even not-so-good ones. They become a great comfort. On a lighter note, just because those loved ones are gone, doesn't mean they suddenly become angels when they lived! One piece of advice even though you didn't ask... keep your sense of humor, you'll need it.

Betty (70's) Smile, laugh, sing, share and dance in my mind. Pray, cry, make some quiet time in my day and share with fellow believers.

❖ ❖ ❖

How are the friends you have made late in life different from the friends you made when you were younger?

Sherri (20's) I am more open to people of different backgrounds, demographics, goals.

Kylie (40's) I think my friendships were less calculated when I was younger and simply who I was hanging around with or even who was attracted to me rather than I to them. I am now becoming more calculated with whom I spend time with and why. I am trying to have healthier relationships. I think as I have gotten older I have become more picky with my time.

Charlotte (60's) To be equal, to be mutual, to make sure that I count too! Adult-to-Adult, to have win-win relationships. Friends are striving for nurturing themselves therefore they nurture me, self-affirming and are healthy for me.

Paige (60's) Old friends share your history, new ones do not have the history, know your mother, father, sisters, husbands, children, etc...

Lorraine (60's) I'm not sure they are. I think I am the different one and my choices are different. My old friends accept me for what I am in spite of what I am. They are precious and very dear to me. We share mutual respect and admiration, compassion and do not judge. My new friends seem to be interested in why I am the way I am, my old friends know and love me anyway.

Betty (70's) When I was young I could "play" a lot harder so it was probably based on who was fun to be with. As I got older I still liked people who were fun to be with but I look way below the surface now. I ask myself what kind of person are they and do we share the same faith commitment, are they loyal etc.

❖ ❖ ❖

How does medicare, medicaid and social security work?

Lorraine (60's) You mean someone really knows?

Betty (70's) Not good enough!

❖ ❖ ❖

" ... our ability to attach meanings to events requires being quiet, building spaces for reflection, and listening with open hearts to what God has to say to us. Only then can we ask the right questions of ourselves, questions, which help us, understand the paths we need to follow."

–Darcy

" Every single day I smile and think about how fortunate I am, how thankful I am, that I have the education and training to be able to have so much freedom in my work life."

–Kameron

What would you have done differently after age 65?

Lorraine (60's) I don't know, but this year is the big 65 and I can't wait to find out!

Betty (70's) What I'm trying to do – laugh more, complain less, love more, criticize less, enjoy the gift of each new day.

❖ ❖ ❖

Is there a drastic change in energy from the 50's to 60's? What changes did you make in your lifestyle to adapt or limit this?

Betty (70's) Heck no! 50 & 60 are still "young." Enjoy and ask me when I'm 80 or 90.

❖ ❖ ❖

What are your dreams?

Sherri (20's) To be content in all important areas: career, marriage, friends.

Adrian (30's) To improve inter race relations in the US, especially between black and white citizens.

Kylie (40's) I have a hard time distinguishing between dreams and goals. I dreamed of having a cabin, pursued it and through the grace of God got it.

Betty (70's) My dream is to see all my grandchildren graduate from high school – maybe even college. In other words to see them become young women and men. That would be a real gift.

❖ ❖ ❖

Will there ever be a day that people stop killing over religious views?

Sherri (20's) Probably not.

Adrian (30's) No.

Kylie (40's) Heaven.

Mary (40's) I don't believe so.

Betty (70's) Not until we all change.

❖ ❖ ❖

How do mothers/daughters maintain a close personal relationship yet respects each other's boundaries?

Sue (20's) Mothers must STOP NAGGING!!!

Kylie (40's) I think that is ever changing and evolving as they grow. I think being aware of changes, and moving through that together. I think if there is genuine respect boundaries will hold up. I think if we have boundary issues with our daughters or mothers, then we have boundary issues as a whole with ourselves and need to address those personally.

Lorraine (60's) It becomes easier as we grow older, I think. Respect is respect at any age. Love is love and there is nothing greater than that between a mother and child. It is easier if you remember that they have made their own choices and those are not necessarily a reflection, good or bad, on you as a parent, but individual life choice of their own. We should accept and respect those choices.

Paige (60's) A mother loves her daughter more than the daughter loves her mother.

Alice (60's) Offer advise ONLY when asked for it. Be available and a good listener when necessary or requested.

❖ ❖ ❖

Do parents know what their children are thinking, not necessarily doing, although important as well?

Sherri (20's) I would say that parents have incredible intuition, but no, in general, parents don't know the intricacies.

❖ 121 ❖

Karrie (20's) I believe I know what my child is thinking and I often ask her what she is thinking. My talking to her like she is my friend rather than just a child, she is able to be open with me and we have wonderful conversations.

Kylie (40's) I think this is impossible, because whenever I try to second-guess what my children are thinking I realize I am imposing my own thoughts and values on them. Instead of worrying what they are thinking I think we need to adopt a policy of listening more. When I approach a conversation with a genuine heart to listen I hear so much more.

I also think this is a generational thing. Each generation has different values associated with it, and we need to be open to the values communicated to our kids to understand their points of view.

Mary (40's) If you are in touch with your kids and talk to them like they matter I think you know.

Lorraine (60's) Not all the time, sometimes not at all! When they are young, teens, it's easier to know if you can remember how you felt... they don't feel any different than we did! I have always kept those tumultuous times in the forefront of my memory, so I could relate to my children when they reached that time of raging hormones and the feeling that my parents, especially my mother, knew nothing at all, only to realize that they (she) knew me only too well... On the occasions when I said I knew how they felt, I really did know.

Paige (60's) To this day I know exactly what my kids are thinking and what is bothering them. I just know it. They do not always know what I am thinking, though... you would think they would by now!

Alice (60's) Only when they want to show these thoughts or activities. Best not to second-guess.

" I cannot believe that I actually said that I would
not ask for any advice. Advice is what I absolutely
needed."
–Diana

" I have learned to not shy away from my
feelings, that feelings are neutral as long
as I am aware of them I can then choose
how to react or act on them."
–Kylie

Betty (70's) We like to think we do but does anyone really know what is inside another's head.

❖ ❖ ❖

Do parents know what their children are feeling?

Karrie (20's) I also believe that I know what my child is feeling, for the same reasons I feel I know what she is thinking. When I notice a particular expression on her face I can usually tell how she is feeling or what she is thinking. To reinforce the situation I will ask her what she is feeling or thinking. This way we can communicate with each other and she feels comfortable sharing her feelings and thoughts with me at any given time.

Kylie (40's) Again, sometimes. I think we know when something is wrong or bothering them, but until we engage in an active dialogue we really don't know what they are feeling. I think what is hard as they grow up, we spend so much time when they are younger associating changes in behavior with physical needs, then it switches to emotional needs and we are not always ready to handle that.

Lorraine (60's) Not all the time. Sometimes you can see it in their eyes or hear it in their voices if you listen. Sometimes it will break your heart, other times your heart will nearly burst with pride, and still others will make you profoundly sad.

Paige (60's) I know what they are feeling, but I don't always know exactly why.

Alice (60's) Not until the feelings are shared by the "children."

Betty (70's) Sometimes we come close. The most important thing is to have "them" feel they are loved and accepted by us.

❖ ❖ ❖

Why can't we treat others how we would like them to treat us?

Sherri (20's) Because we are selfish and usually allow ourselves a longer leash than we do others.

Karrie (20's) We can treat others how we would like them to treat us. We just need to open our hearts and minds. There is no reason to treat others differently than we would like to be treated. Sure there are people who will always be rude or unkind and maybe eventually they will change. If they do not change that doesn't mean that we can have act the same? What we can do is treat them how we would like to be treated and hope that it touches them in some way or another.

Kylie (40's) Great question and a motto we should try to live by, I try! Perhaps too many people don't really know themselves.

Lorraine (60's) Because we are human but we can continue to strive to be that way. I was lucky, I grew up being taught that from the time I was able to listen and understand. I heard that all my young life and continued that to my own children. I don't always succeed, but I always keep trying.

Alice (60's) We feel more vulnerable and less confident in sharing all feelings. We can treat others how we'd like them to treat us but we have no control over how they treat us.

Betty (70's) Probably because deep down we are all self-centered.

❖ ❖ ❖

Tell me about your feelings and your life?

Sherri (20's) I'm anxious, excited, lonely, stimulated, happy.

Betty (70's) I would love to but that would fill a book. I don't think anyone could do that in one sentence unless you just said–deep–full.

❖ ❖ ❖

I would like to ask younger families do they know what they are thinking when they are keeping their kids too busy? Do they know what is on their kid's minds?

Kylie (40's) I think we approach this with great intentions, thinking that if we expose our kids to this and that they will find themselves. But I think you hit a point as a family when you say this is nuts... so I think if you are having too many meals outside of the home that will indicate enough is enough and you need to step back a bit. I also think when you are yelling too much at the kids it's an indicator that you need to pull back.

❖ ❖ ❖

I would like to ask those that are policy makers what are they thinking in regards to media?

Kylie (40's) This is a great question, and larger than that. In fact how do we all hold ourselves accountable in what we do as a living and how does that effect society as a whole?

Paige (60's) No matter what the media reports the conservatives will complain unless it is on a conservative radio or TV station. The liberals are not quite so bad. They are always dealing with nuance and trying to figure it all out.

Betty (70's) I would like to ask them also.

❖ ❖ ❖

Has the struggle for financial success overshadowed everything else?

Sherri (20's) No, and hopefully never.

Adrian (30's) No. I decided long ago that I had to decide that enough was enough. I have always lived below my means, whatever means I have had. And sometimes, those means were pretty few. But there are ways to live without debt.

Lynn (30's) Yes, it has because the cost of living is so high, we have postponed putting off having children, because I wanted to be a stay home mom and now it is too late. Now I am at the point where I could stay home but feel that I might not be able to get pregnant.

Kylie (40's) No, but as I look back I should have been willing to accept a few more "No's" rather than charging it on my credit card to get the immediate satisfaction. I think I have put too much focus on comfort in materialism rather than God.

Betty (70's) I think it is trying hard to. Praise for those who recognize where to put their focus.

❖ ❖ ❖

Where is the caring for one human being over the other?

Kylie (40's) I see it all the time in the church, in friendship, in family. Perhaps if you cannot find it, it is because you are looking in the wrong places.

Betty (70's) It is in a person's heart if it is there at all. Many many people really care for others. That is where it has to begin – with each person.

❖ ❖ ❖

Wants to know what in your life has made you content or unhappy and how did you respond to these situations? And did you share the joys or sorrows with others?

Kylie (40's) When I look back at what has made me happy it has always been relationships, as I also look back at what has really made me sad, it too has been relationships. I think the philosophy of risking love is true. We cannot go through the good without going through the bad. I guess when you are in the good. Know it, share it, enjoy it, and thank God for it. Be very generous! Build a support system during the good times! When you are going through the bad times, hold on, as they say, "man the jib!" Do not sway; trust, pray, have faith, Jeremiah 29:11, claim God's promises to you, and gather your friends to surround you, to help you pull through and ask for their help. Don't do it alone. And don't give up. Surround yourself with stories of hope!

❖ ❖ ❖

What is the secret to success?

Paige (60's) Know yourself. Find peace with God and your family.

❖ ❖ ❖

I would ask any age could you live/have lived without him?

Paige (60's) Finally I am. I was obsessed with having a man and that was my downfall. Being married is not the key to happiness.

Betty (70's) Without who??? Without my husband – I have had to as we all learn to do with Gods help. Without God – no I could not live without His help and compassion.

❖ ❖ ❖

Do you feel like a sham sometimes at work? Are you all as goal-oriented as you seem or when you shut your door is e-mail sometimes all that you can handle?

Sherri (20's) Sure, but that's natural.

Mary (40's) Yes and on those days that is all I handle – we can't all be superwomen everyday.

❖ ❖ ❖

Do you feel secure as a single person?

Sherri (20's) Yes, because I am young. My answer would be different if I weren't 24.

" I would like to live my live over starting as a young child. I would remember never to take life for granted."
–Karrie

" Followed my dreams. People have often thought I was crazy or rash for making some of the career and life choices I've made, but I've always followed my dreams."
–Kate

Penny (40's) Somewhat. From many angles I feel very secure, but culture tells us otherwise which I find stressful.

Mary (40's) Yes.

Paige (60's) Yes, except for money issues.

Betty (70's) Yes.

❖ ❖ ❖

Younger woman with preschool children: How do you manage having so many roles, full-time childcare, wife, homemaker, possibly even outside-the-home career?

Mary (40's) Some days I have it all together and some days it seems as it will all unravel – I take advantage of those "good" days.

❖ ❖ ❖

Older woman: What has kept your relationship good with your son(s) and or daughter(s)?

Paige (60's) By letting go of expectations. Being truly (authentically) happy when they call you. Not transferring guilt because you want something from them. Being respectful of their time and demands in life… then what you get in return is genuine.

Betty (70's) Unconditional love, always being the encourager, not complaining and staying out of their business and private lives.

❖ ❖ ❖

Older woman: What do you do, if you discover that you don't really like the person that your child is choosing to marry or has married?

Paige (60's) Respect your child for picking that person and be ready to support him/her if you were "right" and things fall apart. Never ever say or indicate, "I told you so." This does not hold true for a teenager… then do everything within reason to help the child understand the dangers in his/her choice.

Betty (70's) PRAY It is our child's choice not ours. With God's help we can grow to love and accept them. However, if it is drastic situation then as a parent I believe we should suggest steps that they can take to find out for themselves that it may not be a good match.

❖ ❖ ❖

How do you handle critical people?

Sherri (20's) You extract the truth from what they say and then you ignore the rest. You are also free to dislike them and not respect them if their words are motivated by ill will.

Mary (40's) I try not to be around them

Paige (60's) Not easy... I try really hard to try and analyze them and why they have to be critical. What is their reason for doing so?

Betty (70's) Gently remind them that we are not perfect and help them to see some of the good points about the person or situation.

❖ ❖ ❖

Do you find it difficult to balance health with work?

Paige (60's) Yes, you have to schedule walks/workouts in your day as if an appointment.

❖ ❖ ❖

Do you find it difficult to create new support groups when moving from your home state?

Sherri (20's) Yes, I can't imagine how difficult it would be if I weren't in a campus setting.

Paige (60's) Yes, Yes, Yes... and it gets harder the older you are...

Betty (70's) No.

❖ ❖ ❖

Do you have any advice for getting your husband to respect you as much as they do their mothers and establishing yourself as a the matriarch of your nuclear family?

Sherri (20's) This problem probably has a lot to do with what the mother-in-law might think/say about the new mother. I'd start there.

Mary (40's) Beat the hell out of him – he'll listen sooner or later (sorry, just kidding). You can't MAKE someone respect you – they either do or they don't.

Paige (60's) Takes time... age will earn you that title if you are wise and not expect...

❖ ❖ ❖

What is the one thing you would change in America?

Sherri (20's) Our values.

Penny (40's) That people stop being angry and yelling at each other. The antagonism is rampant in politics and media. This is very sad to me.

Mary (40's) Bring back prayer to schools.

Betsy (50's) I would like to see a greater understanding and acceptance of children.

Paige (60's) The polarization and negativity in politics. The inability of the American public to see through the attacks on candidates. It is absolutely overwhelming to see how a campaign can ruin a candidate by the "spin" and make another seem god-like by the "spin."

❖ ❖ ❖

How do you deal with controlling people?

Mary (40's) I try to control them right back.

Paige (60's) It is hard for me. I still think "they" are right. I have to realize it is their problem and let go of others thinking they are right.

Betty (70's) Quietly stand on my own two feet. It is a difficult place to find your self in but we do not have to be controlled. Many times people are unaware that they are controlling and don't realize how unpleasant that trait is... They are indeed difficult to befriend or work with.

❖ ❖ ❖

Younger Woman: Do you feel like we live in a "good" world and, if so, what helps you feel that way?

Sherri (20's) Yes, because of my youth and the opportunities for change it represents.

❖ ❖ ❖

Younger Woman: What did your parents do that helped you develop some of your better qualities?

Sherri (20's) They were unbelievably generous with their time, support, care, and finances.

❖ ❖ ❖

40 or older: How do you keep from worrying all the time about your own health/mortality and the health and happiness of your children?

Mary (40's) I can't – I need the answer to that question!

❖ ❖ ❖

40 or older: What have you done to raise children who are decent human beings who care about themselves and others?

Betsy (50's) I think this is a daily task. You have to respect the child at each one of his/her stages. You have to encourage open dialogue so the child has the opportunity to reason through acceptable/unacceptable behavior, and so that the child has a chance to express her/himself, and grow from self-knowledge. I think it's the only way to create a pattern the child can follow for life. You have to make them think before they act, and they can do this from an early age. You have to accept that your child may have a different perspective and needs than yours – you don't have to impose yours on him/her. You have to set the example by being decent and caring yourself. This is what I've done, I am almost finished 'growing' my son, and it seems to be paying off.

❖ ❖ ❖

Older Woman: What do you value the most in your life?

Betty (70's) My relationship with my Lord and my relationship with my family.

❖ ❖ ❖

How can you make mother/daughter relationships stronger?

Sherri (20's) Grow from parent: child to parent: adult.

❖ ❖ ❖

What is your relationship like with your grandmother/mother/ daughter?

Sherri (20's) No relationship at all.

❖ ❖ ❖

What are your feelings about yourself and your life?

Sherri (20's) I am still struggling to maintain a consistent sense of positivity.

❖ ❖ ❖

70 or older: What in your life has made you content or unhappy?

Betty (70's) Realizing that God created me and has always had a plan for my life. True happiness is not about having "things." You will never have enough stuff!!!! And in the end what is stuff – NOTHING. New or bigger houses, new or better clothes does not bring true contentment. To spend time with the Lord, to study His word and understand it draws you into a relationship that is the answer. As we age we realize that more and more. We are never alone when we have the Lord and that is when we find happiness and contentment.

❖ ❖ ❖

Other answers to unasked questions

Liz (30's) I guess all I would say is that I'm so glad that as I get older I have become more accepting and grateful of people. We all need many second chances, third chances... the older I get the less I think it's about getting things right and more about just loving and bearing with each other. Lots harder to live that way but lots better.

Darcy (60's) It's not what happens to you, but what you do with what happens to you. It's not what actually happens, but what you perceive as happening. It's not the event, but the meaning attached to the event.

I would add that our ability to attach meanings to events requires being quiet, building spaces for reflection, and listening with open hearts to what God has to say to us. Only then can we ask the right questions of ourselves, questions, which help us, understand the paths we need to follow.

❖ ❖ ❖

" I guess all I would say is that I'm so glad that as I get older I have become more accepting and grateful of people. We all need many second chances, third chances... the older I get the less I think it's about getting things right and more about just loving and bearing with each other. Lots harder to live that way but lots better."

-Liz

spaces of connection

As a visual artist, words carry meaning to me when represented in physical forms. So as I read the letters and stories of these women, my eyes view a Jackson Pollack style painting. The brush strokes on the canvas intertwine with varying degrees of weight, density and are saturated with rich color and bold hues. Sometimes the strokes are firm and deliberate, while other strokes resemble timid spaces and marks of resound. When I view a collection of Pollack's work I am able to see similarities and identify common themes, but when I look at each piece separately I see distinct shapes, which mark their uniqueness, individual characteristics, and meaning.

To me Jackson's paintings are a metaphor for women's conversations. From a distant place the weaving in and out of sound simply adds texture to spaces and time. However, when I move closer into the conversations and hear the distinction between the rhythms that form words I become transformed and mesmerized by the pattern in which these tones create meaning. It is in these spaces of meaning that I am interested in. In these conversations in which women inform, determine, direct, and influence each other's lives. These tones, patterns, textures, and sounds talk about husbands, children, education, faith, elderly parents, exercise, mothers, sisters, friends, careers, co-workers, boyfriends, cooking, poverty, depression, adventure, travel, goals, loss, books, and money. In the same conversation we may have traveled to Europe, married our best friends, said good-bye to a loved-one, decided whom to vote for, and changed our point-of-view on God. As we gather together in conversation we encourage, inspire, relate, and respect each other. In conversation we are compassionate, angry, concerned, and evaluate our various topics with mixed emotions of tears, laughter, joy, and sorrow. It is in these spaces of meaning that we work through our past, live in the present, and move forward into our future.

—*Karen's Reflection*

acknowledgements

This book of conversations happened because of the women who shared their stories, their questions and their answers. It is to these women, our friends, we thank. The honesty and the interest each shared of her journey have culminated in this gathering of conversations. We have changed the names to maintain privacy, but we know who each and every one of you is and we thank you. It is because of you this book has developed.

*"Laugh at yourself. Be ageless in your love for the
companionship of others."*
— ROBERTA

. . .

*" It has taken awhile to dismiss the feelings of guilt over falling asleep
in the middle of the afternoon or watching a movie instead of
doing the laundry! Or reading into the wee hours of the morning...
or having a glass of wine for no reason except to enjoy it...
how delightful! I can enjoy!"*
— LORRAINE

. . .

*"... concentrate on the areas you have some control over and
let go of the areas you cannot control."*
— CHARLOTTE

. . .

"Expect NOTHING but their love and you will reap rewards."
— PAIGE

. . .

*"To live a life of integrity knowing in your heart you have
done your very best."*
— BETTY

. . .

*"I have discovered that the best things in life, have happened
without my knowledge, input, or meddling."*
— CARLIE

. . .

*" I would have dumped my college boyfriend the day I knew he wasn't
the right person for me. I wasted time and effort."*
— MARSELLA

. . .

"If you can be honest with yourself as well as all others you will, ultimately, have a good life."
— GENE

. . .

"Love is love and there is nothing greater than that between a mother and child. It is easier if you remember that they have made their own choices and those are not necessarily a reflection, good or bad, on you as a parent, but individual life choice of their own. We should accept and respect those choices."
— LORRAINE

. . .

"Don't do it alone. And don't give up. Surround yourself with stories of hope!"
— KYLIE

. . .

"Things happen, some good, some bad. When you have a bad experience, try to learn from it, and then move on. There are always options! Many times we blind ourselves to choices right in front of us. Reach out; help usually comes from the most unexpected place. If you have a positive experience – ENJOY IT – keep it as a memory to use during a bad time."
— SALLY

. . .

"Love yourself, every imperfect part of you, see life as a journey – not a goal line."
— SUSAN

. . .

"I have love to spare, which often causes me great pain."
— LAURA

. . .

"... most of us are struggling with one thing or another, and we could probably stand to share more of that with the people around us."
— LAURA

. . .

*"Don't put on hold the things that you ultimately want...
it may be too late."*
— LYNN

. . .

"... don't be so afraid to make a mistake, it will happen no matter what, in ways that you had no idea. That is just the nature of life. And trust that as long as we live through Christ's lense the journey will be good."
— KYLIE

. . .

"I would like to tell another woman that until she feels good about herself, life is a compromise and disappointing."
— ALICE

. . .

"Pray, cry, call a good friend."
— ADRIAN

. . .

"Acceptance is a difficult thing to learn, very difficult when you are young, the older you get, the more you realize that if it is meant to be it will be."
— LORRAINE

. . .

"Can anyone give me some advice on how to do this and how to keep going every day?"
— DIANA

. . .